CRICKET IN THE BACKBLOCKS

By the same author:

Policeman in Africa, The Book Guild 1997
Policeman in Palestine, Edward Gaskell 1995

CRICKET IN THE BACKBLOCKS

Colin Imray

The Book Guild Ltd
Sussex, England

The Book Guild Ltd.
25 High Street
Lewes, Sussex

First published 1998

Set in Times
Typesetting by
Southern Reproductions (Sussex)
Crowborough, Sussex
Printed in Great Britain by
Bookcraft (Bath) Ltd,
Avon

A catalogue record for this book is
available from the British Library

ISBN 1 85776 287 8

Dedicated
to
Cricket
and
to all Cricketers
wherever they
may be.

'Cricket civilizes people and creates good gentlemen. I want everyone to play cricket in Zimbabwe. I want ours to be a nation of gentlemen.'

ROBERT MUGABE

CONTENTS

ACKNOWLEDGEMENTS

Once again, as with my two earlier books, my thanks and appreciation for his careful editing go to my friend H.V.F. (Victor) Winstone. Without his professional guidance I would never have been able to get off the literary floor. I owe much too to my friend Ann Shand, who word-processed the entire manuscript.

For help in my researches into cricket facts and figures, I am much indebted to the following:

The curator of the Marylebone Cricket Club at Lords, for information on the Harlequins Cricket Club and other matters.

Mr John Keegan, the Defence Secretary of the *Daily Telegraph,* for replying most helpfully to my query about the Regimental Officers' Mess.

Barry England's theatrical production, *Conduct Unbecoming,* which made me think back deeply upon aspects of Services mess life that I have encountered.

Mr J.W. McKenzie of McKenzie's cricket book shop at Ewell, Epson, Surrey, who was most helpful in finding for me books on cricket matters – and in particular a book on Worcester cricket, which gave me valuable information on the Foster family.

My friend Major Barry Lane, for his help in making useful contacts.

Mr Osborne, the librarian at the County Cricket Ground, Hove, was good enough to give me some most helpful assistance in my researches.

Finally, I am grateful to my son, R.P. (Robert) Imray for

his encouragement and for access to his set of *Wisden's Almanack.*

PRELUDE

I was at school at Malvern College, having arrived there, goodness knows how, via the Common Entrance Examination.

However, I was a scholastic disaster. I failed, not once but at the second attempt as well, to gain the all-important School Certificate, which was the elementary testimonial – the piece of paper that all aspiring boys and girls take in their stride as a matter of course.

At that time, School Certificate was divided into groups. If you failed in one group, you failed the entire business. I was triumphant, and even got distinctions in English, History, Latin, French, Geography and Scripture. Lamentably, however, the group or groups comprising Arithmetic, Algebra, Geometry, Chemistry and Physics were hopelessly beyond me.

It wasn't Malvern's fault; it was just my own personal make-up, there was probably a screw loose somewhere. Arithmetic, despite the ministrations of a Miss Misfit in much earlier years, always paralysed my thinking, and in the vital examination I reduced all the set problems to multiplication and long division, but my calculations became so involved that they went off the page and I left them lying there in limbo, as it were. Algebra, with its 'As and Bs, Xs and Ys' was anathema to me. It seemed to me to be slightly rude, and I preferred to leave it alone. I believe I offered up a completely blank page. A later acquaintance of mine always boasted that, faced with the same problem, he had boldly written across the paper 'Balls', which for a schoolboy was impolite to say the least, and I gathered that he failed the examination.

Geometry, too, was beyond me, but I tried to improvise – I drew an enormous triangle labelled 'British Empire' (in which I firmly believed) and within it, rather laboriously with my geometry set, I drew triangles and circles depicting – in the middle – India, the cornerstone of the Empire, which I coloured in deep red. I portrayed in lesser designs historical events such as Livingstone's African journeys, the attempts to find the source of the Nile, the 'Boxer' episode in China, the 'Great Game' in Central Asia, and so on. I hoped thus to persuade the examiner of the ingenuity of my method, but that ploy failed too.

Physics I put firmly behind me as being unworthy of my attention; I believe I thought it was something to do with physical training, which I never cared for. As for Chemistry, there had been an episode when in the laboratory, over a Bunsen burner, I mixed together two substances that didn't like each other. There was a loud report, and everything ascended to the ceiling. All in the room, including Mr Berridge the master, dived for cover, and I was left standing there with no eyebrows and a bald patch where the peak of my hair used to be.

In later years, visiting Malvern, I paid a pilgrimage to that laboratory and there, sure enough, the still unwhitewashed ceiling bore a familiar yellowish mark. Anyhow, I had been rightly thrown out of the science block, such as it then was.

Reporting for cricket to Charles Fiddian Green, the cricket master who, after winning his Cambridge Blue had played for both Warwickshire and Worcestershire, I was asked, 'What on earth have you been doing?'

In time-honoured schoolboy fashion, I said, 'Nothing, sir.'

'Right,' he said, 'get over into the nets and do some bowling.' He clearly wasn't impressed by what he saw.

I recall two Mathematics masters. One was the excellent Frank Roberts, who struggled with me for a while, but finally wrote in the report sent to my despairing parents, 'I cannot teach this boy.' The other was Walter Lowe, an old Malvernian, who had an astonishing record of prowess at cricket, football, golf and athletics, but I doubt whether he was a great teacher of Maths. Towards the end of the period he would line us up outside the classroom door, and when the bell went he'd wave his hands and shout 'Away', and he'd be first off the mark.

I was, of course, undeniably 'dim', and as a new boy I was always late and always getting lost. After my Prep School everything seemed so vast and impersonal, and hostility seemed to encompass me at every turn.

The school porter, Gunster, was my only friend. After all classes had assembled and my own bunch had somehow disappeared into the blue, I would be be wandering around the deserted corridors, probably having lost my books, trying to find where I belonged. I would seek out the porter – 'Oh please, Mr Gunster, can you tell me where Mr X's class is this morning?' – and somehow I would get there halfway through a lesson and be received less than enthusiastically.

To this very day I have nightmare dreams of my early Malvern days.

Sergeant-Major Robinson, with his waxed moustaches, was of the 'Old School'. Late as usual one day, I reported to him. 'Please, Sergeant-Major, I thought . . .' He looked at me rather as Lord Kitchener looked at the nation in 1915. 'Understand this; only five people in this world are allowed to think, one is 'is Majesty King George V, son of 'is Blessed Majesty King Edward VII, Gawd bless 'im.' (At which he sprang to attention and saluted.) 'The others are the 'eadmaster, Captain Elliott (who commanded the OTC), Mr 'olmes (E.R.T. Erroll-Holmes, who was then captain of Cricket), and myself.' By this time I had become aware of a strong aroma of beer in the vicinity of the Sergeant-Major.

Not surprisingly, when I left Malvern in the summer of 1927, I wasn't much use to anybody in that climate of approaching economic slump. I was 'placed' with a firm in the City that acted as agents for a company in Malaya, which was in effect 'pig-in-the-Middle' between European manufacturers and Chinese and Indian traders in the East. It was devoutly hoped by everybody, including myself, that the time might arise when I would be shipped off there, out of sight and mind.

As a matter of fact, I was really rather ashamed of myself. All my friends seemed to have done so much better and taken the tiresome business of school very much in their stride.

Although I failed to make the grade at school cricket, the seed had been planted in me at an early age and had begun to germinate, and I believe I can say that I got the 'mystic feel' of the game whilst still at school. After all, the seven cricketing Fosters were all educated at Malvern. So *Floreat* Malvern Cricket.

I have tried to write without too much gravity about places that I knew some 60 years ago as a very young man. But I can't resist the thought that the almost vacuous political philosophy of the colonial regimes I knew – and vastly enjoyed – in the inter-war years, led in the case of Singapore to one of the greatest military disasters in the long and proud history of the British Empire.

Again, I ask myself how the major setback of four years' Japanese occupation was overcome in such spectacular fashion? Are the British perhaps an entirely illogical yet endlessly resilient people? Was I, during my early years in Singapore and Malaya, in common with all around me, too much immersed in the public-school-dominated ethos of Empire to notice the true significance of what was happening to the ordinary worthwhile people of the place? I hope that my light-hearted story may perhaps give rise to a glimmer of understanding.

My story of 'Cricket in the Backblocks' commences in the very Imperial setting of Singapore and Malaya during the period 1928/1931. And I have continued on through Palestine, Gold Coast and Kenya.

But, of course, memories go back constantly to the real thing. When you watched the greats at work in the middle and listened to stories about their shining moments, your own world of bat and ball seems to fade into a hazy indifference. Yet it was a very real world of camaraderie and fun; and of achievement that is worthy of record, so long as it isn't confused with the real mastery of the flannelled gods.

First, though, I must dwell in those gods – or at any rate on those I was able to see at work – before my personal story begins.

I remember one evening spent over a drink with 'Bo' Brown. Bo had captained Northants on several occasions. He said he wasn't a very good cricketer, just good enough to 'stand in' sometimes. However, he had played against W.J. (Tiger) O'Reilly, the Australian wizard, and had been fascinated by the Tiger's technique. On his dining table, with the aid of a set of chessmen, he would demonstrate his hero's field settings, and then go through it all again on his son's blackboard, showing how O'Reilly beguiled batsmen with his unorthodox action, his seemingly innocuous leg-breaks and, just when the batsman thought he had mastered the spin and was reading it correctly, the vicious, unreadable googly; how he lured the enemy into a false sense of security before unleashing a ball against which even the finest batsmen were destined to meet their Waterloo.

I remember the summer of 1919 and my first four county matches at Hove, when Sussex played Yorkshire, Somerset, Kent and Northants.

George Hirst was playing one of his last games for Yorkshire; he only got five and didn't bowl. It was the first of several occasions when I saw the great all-rounder Wilfred Rhodes in action.

I have to refresh my memory with *Wisden* when it comes to the number of runs or wickets, but after 70 or more years the manner of it all is fresh in the memory. In the Somerset encounter, Robert Relf scored 101 for Sussex and 'Farmer' White took nine wickets in the match. For Kent, that giant among all-rounders Frank Woolley made a predictable century, and I can still see him in my mind's eye, bowling his left-arm spinners with that wonderfully graceful high action, and diving like a bird in the slips to take the most astonishing catches. And I mustn't neglect V.W.C. Jupp's 103 for Sussex.

In the following year, I was taken at the age of 11 to Lord's, to see E.P. Hewetson of Shrewsbury, playing for the Rest against Lord's Schools, take 9 wickets for 33. If I am not mistaken, practically all his victims were clean-bowled.

I saw several of the schools matches in the early 1920s, and have a memory of one J.G. Pugh of Rugby, who got 81 and was the only Lord's batsman to show any confidence against Hewetson's speed. For several years he had dominated those encounters. Duleepsinhji of Cheltenham got a century in one match, but by then Hewetson had gone up to Oxford. In 1921, Warwick Armstrong, captain of the all-conquering Australian side of that year, enters my kaleidoscope of cricketing memories, leaning up against the Oval pavilion rails, obviously bored stiff, chewing toffees (or perhaps gum) while his men 'in the middle' played havoc with Surrey. And then, when they came in, there was J.M. (Jack) Gregory, much taller than the rest of them, smiling broadly and sharing a joke with the gatekeeper – no longer the bounding fearsome terror that he'd been to the Surrey batsmen.

And in 1921 I had a prolonged sight of Jack Hobbs in the field. He seemed to have uncanny anticipation in the covers, and moved like lightning to cut off the ball and then make an accurate under-the-shoulder throw straight back at the wicketkeeper (usually Herbert Strudwick). Two years previously I had seen the Master bat for the first time. It was at Lord's against Middlesex; I remember that much. He got a number of effortless runs but, to my chagrin, he made a rare mistake and was caught. It seemed to me that whoever caught him was guilty of a tasteless enterprise.

Then there are some uncharted memories. I recall the ungainly, though remarkably effective, Philip Mead of

Hampshire, whom I saw somewhere making a lot of runs rather slowly. Then there was the valiant Maurice Tate of Sussex, bowling accurately and interminably, and with obvious good humour, although he wasn't taking wickets. I recall too the enormous pressure of work on Bill Hitch and Tom Rushby of Surrey, who were then the only effective bowlers the County had, except for P.G.H. (Percy) Fender, who bowled when he felt like it. There was Fender's miraculous slip-catching to savour, and Andy Sandham of Surrey, Hobb's opening partner, standing by the Oval pavilion rails, shuffling into position for an enormous skier and taking it with both hands resting on his right shoulder, to his very obvious relief.

I owed my frequent appearances in the Oval Pavilion to one of my prep school masters, K.E. King, and his father, who must have been very old indeed and had clearly become one of 'The Critics' as well as being a generous benefactor of cricket among Surrey members. 'Kingo' used to collect parties of us schoolboys, whether still at the prep school or later, and take us to the Oval under his father's banner. The whole thing had become a kind of pilgrimage and had an almost religious aura. I recall an occasion when a white-moustached gentleman was speaking to somebody in the row ahead of us. The sepulchral whisper came down the line from Kingo – 'A.C. Maclaren.' And there came a day when we were actually introduced to the Reverend C.I. Thornton.

There was always an end of season match at the Oval – Champion County versus Rest of England. Somehow in those early days I managed to get to most of these encounters. I was there in 1919 to see a century by Jack Hobbs against Yorkshire, and then a double century by Hobbs again in 1920, against Middlesex. In 1921 there was the incredible dismissal of Hubert Ashton, playing against Middlesex. He had made 27 when he lashed one very hard round to square leg. I looked for the boundary, but 'Young Jack' Hearne had taken it quite imperturbably, and Ashton was out.

I was one of the fortunate schoolboys who were present in 1924 to see a remarkable display by Woolley (202) and Chapman (74), both left-handers. They lashed the formidable Yorkshire bowling Waddington, Robinson, Macaulay, Rhodes and Kilner. Rhodes, in particular suffered badly. E.R. Wilson, the captain, was clearly trying to take him off, but the indomitable old senior professional was equally clearly saying, 'Just one more over, sir, and I'll have 'em.'

One of the last of my schoolboy memories takes me to Hove in 1925, when Australia played Sussex. Arthur Mailey and Clarrie Grimmett bowled – I believe unchanged for the two hours before lunch – in a deadly accurate display of spin bowling.

I became, in short, at a very early age, entranced by cricket. I came to love the game and all the Princes of it, fair or foul; and to wish – oh how I wished – that I was better at it. But like everyone who ever played the great game, at any level, I had my moments.

My own experiences of cricket were far removed from such hallowed places. But the game – and other happenings – in jungle clearings and on improvised sandy wickets – will I hope interest a reader or two, and perhaps provoke an occasional laugh.

1

Cricket Charisma

A discerning eye will observe even in the stride of a cricketer a certain swagger that identifies him, while his speech – if you know him well enough – will say 'cricketer', every inch. And – I must say it – there exists from youth to old age among a few who have cricket in their blood, a permanent streak of adolescence.

Most, though certainly not all, are very nice people, these cricketers, but perhaps the adolescence to which I refer contains a certain vein of snobbery towards lesser lights who haven't been able to find, or have been denied access to, the magic of the sacred turf.

The Englishman has been, and probably still is, despite the end of colonial days, a great traveller. Set down in the most unlikely terrain, he would, in my day at least, start thinking cricket. He would dream nostalgically of days when a few runs or wickets or a good catch earned him the applause of fellow players; perhaps – if he was sufficiently eminent – a return to the pavilion to the accompaniment of the applause of the crowd. To field, to bowl, to bat; it didn't matter, so long as he was there on the field in good times and bad, saturated in the game's inexplicable mystique. And so he would feel, this alienated Englishman out in the backblocks, that in common decency he must try to impart a little of his strange religion to the locals among whom he had come to live.

Of course, this is all in the past tense. The Empire is over and done with. The students have become the game's worthiest practitioners. But the past is still vivid in my memory, and I find myself ranting on as if nothing has changed.

Without actually letting the colonial peoples into his secret thoughts, the Englishman set them to work (in those days they were usually prisoners from the nearest gaol), hacking a field out of the surrounding bush, or smoothing a stretch of desert sand into a hard surface. He managed to acquire from somewhere the tools of the trade – stumps, bails, balls, bats, pads, gloves – and then he got to work on the bemused natives.

Sometimes, just occasionally, they came up to his expectations, and he would speak delightedly of Mohammed el Faroukhi's development as a useful leg-spinner, or proclaim the footwork of Salifu Grunshie and insist that, given decent schooling, he might easily make a Ranjitsinhji.

Equally, the locals might spurn the blandishments of the crazy Englishman, and he would be liable to find them – to his chagrin – playing football or some other 'inferior' game.

I think I may have been born with cricket 'in' me, or in close proximity. If my father's story is true (I don't remember the occasion), I once had my head patted by none other than Dr W.G. Grace. This remarkable encounter is said to have taken place at Mitcham in Surrey around 1912, when the bearded Master was attending a charity match. The head-patting occurred apparently during the tea interval, when my father was instructing the three-year-old me in the art of the straight bat. Manifestly, to be head-patted by W.G. must sow the seeds of cricket. The flower was to be long delayed in coming to bloom, however. As my mentors used to say later on at Malvern, 'This boy will never make a cricketer; he won't learn, and he's far too impatient.'

However, it happened, I was 'cricketized' from the outset. One of my big memories was a day in Jack Hobbs's shop in Fleet Street. The great man was there, and actually chose a bat for me and autographed it; I was ecstatic.

I have already mentioned that I watched my first four county cricket matches on the Sussex ground at Hove. I saw Sussex at work against Yorkshire, Northants, Kent and Somerset. Oh, the awe and the reverence I had for those white-clad gladiators! And then later on – again at Hove – the gods stood before me.

I was one of a number of fortunate boys being coached at the nets. Harold Larwood was there, because Sussex were playing Nottingham, and he was invited to bowl at us but to keep them on the off-side. And so it was; I was bowled at by the man who was to achieve such cricketing fame and notoriety under Douglas Jardine's captaincy in Australia.

All the same, my Malvern masters were quite right; I never achieved my 'colours' at school, but I did play a lot later on – and with some success – when I came to roost in one or other of the major stations of our former Empire, and I did indeed play my part here and there in carrying cricket into the backblocks.

In the immediate aftermath of World War One, I was considered 'delicate'. I remember being confined to bed for some weeks, or even months, and covering the walls of my room with photographs from the recently published *Cricketer.* I must have recovered a certain robustness by 1921, however, for I remember clearly the Australian tour of that year (I would have been 12 years old) and seeing the tall, bounding Jack Gregory who, along with Ted McDonald and his glorious fluent bowling action, crashed through the best of England's formidable batting line-up. That Australian XI was only beaten at Eastbourne and Scarborough, in the last two matches of the tour. According to *Wisden,* Hubert Ashton, a Cambridge Blue, was one of the very few to master the demon Australian bowling. I was, myself, to play against Ashton many years later in Palestine. I have recounted elsewhere something of this*.

---

* *Policeman in Palestine,* published by Edward Gaskell, 1995

My grandfather had created a family holiday place at Seaford, within striking distance of the Hove County Cricket ground. The place was full of boys' prep schools. If you were a good cricketer, and especially a Blue, you were much sought-after as a member of staff. For a miserable stipend and your keep during termtime, you might find it a pleasant way of life to become a master at such an institution, particularly if you had a little extra on top of your abysmal salary. So Seaford cricket never lacked talent. Even during the long summer holidays, some of these people whose names cricket-wise added lustre to Seaford, would be around to play with us up on that airy, wind-swept ground at the nearby village of Blatchington.

It was here, under the eagle eye of Mr Sutcliffe, uncle of the immaculate Yorkshire and England opener, Herbert Sutcliffe, that I received my first coaching in the nets. Over the wall at the end of the ground lived a family called Coldstream, and one of the sons, Frank, a large, rangy young man then up at Oxford, was being groomed to bowl fast for Sussex. I watched in awe one day when Herbert Sutcliffe (Sussex must have been playing Yorkshire at Hove), together with the indomitable Maurice Tate and the then Sussex skipper, H.L. Wilson, were putting Frank Coldstream through his paces. He was indeed very fast, but his hobby, as he once told me, was beer, and I don't think he ever made the grade, not even his University Blue.

It was good cricket company up there at Blatchington, and I have never forgotten my pride and joy when, at the age of 16, I was selected to play in one or two minor games for Seaford. In those days, of course, amateurs ruled the game, and the first-class 'gents' were never too proud to be seen on a club ground or wearing a club cap. On at least one occasion we were actually captained by H.L. Wilson himself; he kept a market garden in Seaford.

It was against Newhaven that I first distinguished myself on the greensward. Our last Seaford batsman came in, and we needed 15 to win. Leg-glancing a fast-medium bowler off my toes, I got 12 of the required runs in an arc which ran from about leg slip to backward square, and somehow we won the game. H.L. Wilson was sitting there, watching with a friend – he wasn't playing – and his companion shouted to me, 'Come here, youngster.' Although I didn't then know it, this was V.W.C. Jupp, then playing for Sussex as an amateur. He said, 'Who do you think you are, Ranji, taking them off your feet like that?' Then he added, in an aside to Wilson, 'That young devil might make a batsman.'

H.L. brought me down to earth. 'You won't get anywhere unless you go and clean those filthy boots,' he said.

I suppose I said, 'Yes sir, thank you sir,' or something like it.

I followed the career of Jupp with keen interest after that boyhood encounter. He made eight appearances for England, against Australia, South Africa and the West Indies, and played for Northants as a professional.

Later on I had another brief moment of reflected glory, which I can't resist relating. I played twice – at Hendon and Purley – with Duleepsinhji, a nephew of the great Ranjitsinhji. I can't remember just when this would have been, but I must have been playing for Hampstead Nomads at the time. Certainly Duleep had already played for England, and I well remember him wearing his 'Hawks' (of Cambridge) cap. He was a most modest, charming young man, and said he was always nervous when playing club cricket, because so much was expected of him. However, I recall him making one peerless 50 for us.

2

Singapore

I was certainly not among the brightest and best of all the many young hopefuls who have left their native land for a business career out East.

However, 'influence' had been invoked, and there I was in February 1928 at the age of 19, sailing out of Birkenhead on the Blue Funnel (Alfred Holt) ship SS *Diomed,* bound for Singapore, where I was to join a company in the Straits Settlements, as Malaya was sometimes called. The company acted as middleman between the European manufacturers and Chinese and Indian merchants.

The *Diomed* was a cargo vessel carrying up to 20 passengers. On our trip there were only 12, and I was the sole greenhorn. The talk was always exuberant and larger than life, and I lapped it all up with enormous enthusiasm and gullibility. In the Bay of Biscay we 'caught it' good and true, and for 24 hours the *Diomed* did everything but capsize. I believe that this was the storm Lloyd George experienced on a voyage which followed the Liberals' final demise, and which he talked about ever afterwards. As for me, I stayed on my bunk. There were straps to keep one anchored, and I recall standing alternately on my head and my feet. And then we woke to a perfect day and a flat sea as we skirted the Portuguese coast, and from then on the voyage was pure delight, with Port Said my first sight of the East. I had been told of the Red Sea's blistering heat, but at this time of year it was relatively cool.

Stopping to coal at Perim, near Aden on the Strait of Bab el Mandab, I watched some sailors fishing for shark, and the spectre of these enormous fish impressed me greatly. Then there was the longish haul across the Indian Ocean to Malaya, missing out Colombo, calling at Penang and Port Swettenham before reaching my destination – Singapore. The approach by ship took a long time through palm-fringed islands. Singapore itself, some 15 by 27 miles, is by far the largest of quite a considerable archipelago off the southern tip of the Malay peninsular.

There to meet me was a stout 40-year-old Scot, Mr Maconochie, who was to be my manager. I don't think he was prepared for anyone quite so young and green, but he was very kind to me. He wore white 'ducks' and a pith helmet, called a 'solar topee'. I too had one of these Empire hats, bought in a London store, and I was very proud of it.

In those days the country was divided into two parts. There was the Colony (Straits Settlements) and the FMS (Federated Malay States). The Colony consisted of Singapore, Penang (with Province Wellesley), and Malacca, which was quite a sizeable strip of territory on the west coast. FMS was in fact a loose title that designated the rest of Malaya and included both federated and unfederated states.

The Federation, by treaty in 1896, originally consisted of four states. The remainder were unfederated then, but joined the Federation later. For practical purposes, all the states – though nominally ruled by their Sultans/Rajahs – were under strong British influence ('veiled autocracy' as it has been called) exercised by Political Residents (senior members of the Malayan Civil Service).

The entire territory was administered by a Governor from Singapore. In my time the office was held by Sir Hugh Clifford, very much a star figure among early colonial Governors. Sadly, deteriorating health compelled his retirement from the service shortly after my arrival in Singapore. He was replaced by Sir Cecil Clementi, whom I never saw, but there was a story current that his wife made it her personal mission to 'clean up' Singapore, which meant that the 'business' ladies of the town gradually vanished from the scene for the time being.

Of Sir Hugh Clifford, many a story is told. I met a man years later in Britain called Mr Mills (he pretended to have forgotten his own first name), who had been all over the Far East, including Mukden. Having occasion to do some business in Government House, he wandered around its corridors and got lost.

Eventually he knocked on a door and entered. It was Sir Hugh's study and Sir Hugh was at his desk. Undeterred by the somewhat casual nature of the encounter, the two men introduced themselves and sat down to a profitable conversation about the territories, which Mills knew like the back of his hand; he was grilled in great detail about Mukden, a territory that was not especially familiar to colonial administrators of the day.

The Clifford approach was not uncommon in the Colonies. I was to meet later on in Africa with at least two Governors who expected even the most junior members of the administration to keep them informed, and not necessarily to go through the 'right channels'.

Cricket, of course, was high on the Residency's priority list. A senior official, 'Sniffy' Clark, to whom I was introduced in response to my eager questions about cricket, saw to it that I was directed to the right quarter. But my new mentor worked in mysterious ways.

'Sniffy' introduced me to another member of the Service, down from the wilds of Pahang. It was from him that I first heard about the aboriginals of the Malayan jungle, the Sakhai and the Semang. It all gave me a great urge to go up-country and immerse myself in the 'real' Malaya.

Trade throughout Malaya was very largely in the hands of the Chinese, though to a far lesser degree there were Indian stores in very many places. The big European business houses (the 'Merchants') were then in their heyday, with their headquarters at Singapore, Penang or Kuala Lumpur, and branches at most other places. Names easily recalled are Syme Darby, Guthrie's, the Borneo Company, BAT (British American Tobacco Co.), Boustead's, and the APC (Asiatic Petroleum Co.).

These all exercised very considerable influence and, among other virtues, they greatly benefited Malaya's cricket, because recruitment was always very selective, and if you were a cricket – or perhaps a rugger – Blue and prepared to accept a life of heat, mosquitoes and various kinds of fever, you were an automatic choice. My own company was not among the élite, however, and we certainly didn't have any Blues.

Rubber had been introduced into Malaya from Brazil in the early years of British Colonial administration, which had commenced at the instigation of Sir Stamford Raffles in 1819. On the estates up in the FMS (there was very little rubber on Singapore island) the labour force, which meant the 'tappers' of rubber trees, mainly consisted of Tamils from southern India. These people were usually accommodated in what seemed to me later on to be highly insanitary, evil-smelling coolie lines.

But Chinese shops and stores abounded. Indeed, the Chinese predominated in every walk of life – servants, waiters, clerks and everyone else, all seemed to be Chinese, and I was enormously impressed by their capacity for sustained hard work.

I was immediately struck on arrival by the conspicuous absence from view of the Malays themselves. Certainly they didn't seem to appear at all among the trading fraternity, and until I went up-country I had only encountered Malays driving taxis, doing messenger jobs in offices *(Tambies),* or working as fishermen or as gardeners *(kebuns).* I was to learn that, in sharp contrast to the Chinese, the Malay people preferred a less energetic life style, though this, in much later years, was to undergo some dramatic changes.

In those days Singapore had four presentable hotels, and a lot more that were less than presentable. In descending order these were the Europe, where the *Tuan Besars* (the big bosses), who headed the mercantile houses, used to give their Saturday evening parties. Then there was Raffles – very cosmopolitan – whose big feature was the afternoon tea dance. After that came the Adelphi, where they served a marvellous grill and always seemed to put on a glamorous cabaret.

And finally there was the Sea View, out at Katong in exotic surroundings, with lamp-shaded ballroom, swimming pool and palm-fringed outlook. It was said that anything could happen here, and it probably did, though I was too young to notice.

Not so very far away from the middle of Singapore's West End, there was a rapid descent downmarket. The Van Wyk Hotel catered for the sea-going fraternity, and I remember being present when the Dutch manager, who bore a striking resemblance to De Valera, the Irish President, came out with a gun to quell some brawling sailors.

At the Raffles, always impeccably dressed, was the portly, popular, ever-genial Laverton ('Lavvy'), the hotel manager. He was also very much a personality on the Singapore cricket scene.

I soon found the Cricket Club and its long rectangular sports ground (the Padang), and almost immediately became a member. Needless to say, I longed to join the august company in the middle.

For my first week I was quartered at the Adelphi, and was entranced by a Hawaiian cabaret party and the remarkable contortions of several of its young women. In due course I moved to one of the European-run boarding houses. In search of the cheapest possible accommodation, I was to move around to quite a number of these establishments, but finally settled for a fairly sleazy flat on the Orchard Road.

My company's offices were on Collyer Quay, overlooking the sea 'roads' with sampans everywhere. Further along the coastal Straits, steamships were for ever on the move. In the office was an orchidaceous Eurasian girl, Dorothy; I was entranced by her too.

Almost at once my manager, Mr Maconochie, pitched me out into the market to sell 'General Goods' to Chinese retailers.

I was put under the tutelage of a persuasive good-looking Chinese called Swee Leong, who kept talking about 'my wife' (his; I hadn't acquired one). Through him I learnt my way around Singapore and became acquainted with our agents, mainly Chinese *towkays* (merchants), and with our competitors.

Swee Leong was a splendid tutor and guide. I soon picked up the Singapore Malay *lingua franca.* This was essential, because everybody spoke it everywhere, and I achieved a fair grasp of it. I hear that now, years on, it is rarely used in Singapore.

Only a few miles away, across the causeway into what is now Malaysia, the Malay language *Behasa Malayu* is the official tongue; very different from the Chinese-impregnated stuff that we used to speak in Singapore.

I was much helped in my Malay studies by a colleague named Heath, tall, angular and dark-visaged, who ran the Singapore section of our cigarette business. We were agents for Carreras and fought a perpetual losing battle against the formidable BAT.

Heath's grasp of Singapore Malay was complete. He would be visited in the office by a procession of *Towkays,* and they would talk interminably in Malay. I used to listen avidly, and quickly got the feel of the language. I was to see him again in London early in 1932, when we had both become jobless, and afterwards I heard that he had returned to Malaya, where he assisted the Security Forces during the War and was captured by the Japanese. I have often wondered whether he survived.

In the office under Mr Maconochie was the head *kerani,* or clerk, one Hoo Teck. Apart from the manager, nobody ever addressed him unless first spoken to by him. He was a portly, taciturn, revered figure with an encyclopaedic knowledge of everyone and everything in Singapore. He always seemed to be deep in thought, and I was scared stiff of him.

The three others in our section were Ah Tay, a junior clerk who was kicked around by Hoo Teck, and a wretched Malay Tamby aged about 14, Jafaa, who was kicked around by everyone.

The remaining personality was a morose fat Malay Tamby called Hassan, who wouldn't move from his chair unless virtually forced out of it. Even Hoo Teck had trouble with him, and I believe in the end he was given the sack for being bone idle.

The rainy season in those latitudes is quite an experience. Our office was a wooden structured building over a godown (warehouse). It had a long balcony and we overlooked the sea, separated indeed from the sea wall by just the width of a road.

There were times when the rain came down in sheets and one couldn't see much further than a few yards into the 'roads'; it just beat down with enormous intensity. Incredibly there would emerge out of the deluge a wretched rickshaw-man – invariably Chinese – hauling his rickshaw with some passenger under the hood and apron, who nevertheless must have got very wet too.

They say the mortality rate among these rickshaw-men was very high, and I'm not surprised. However, they performed an essential service for those, like myself, who couldn't afford a car. There were plenty of taxis, but the rickshaw was much cheaper and got one to a destination fairly quickly.

I gather that the rickshaw has vanished now from the streets of Singapore, and certainly for the sakes of the unfortunate creatures who had to do the pulling, it's just as well.

On the subject of rain, I remember that within the office at the height of a storm it was impossible to speak, hear or think, on account of the water crashing down on our tin roof. Indeed, we had a number of roof leaks that nobody in my time had bothered about.

Needless to say, from the start of my time in Singapore I had espoused with gusto the pernicious 'chit' system.

One simply signed a chit for everything and paid up – if one could – at the month's end. Of course I got hopelessly out of my depth, and it was nearly a year before I cleared a mounting debt by taking myself very seriously in hand.

Not so very long after my arrival, Mr Maconochie handed me a packet amd told me to take it out to the captain of a coastal ship that lay out in the Roads. I was to hire a sampan, and I did as commanded.

Approaching the companion ladder of the ship, I heard a shocking hubbub from the deck above me – shrieks, screams, yells and then a shot – followed by silence and much groaning. Up the ladder I went with my package, and there on deck I was met with a scene of carnage. Several Chinese were lying around in pools of blood, either dead or nearly so; and there, outside a deckhouse, in his vest and trousers, carrying a revolver, was an enormously fat white man.

Nearby was another body. I felt distinctly queazy, but I went up to the captain – for this was the revolver-carrying white man – handed him the packet and asked for a receipt.

He didn't say much, except to exclaim, 'These people!', but he invited me into his cabin and scribbled a reply, whereupon I departed at speed, somewhat shaken. This, I thought, must be a regular occurrence in these parts, and I must just get used to it.

What had happened was that a Malay had run amock on the deck with his sharp, curved dagger, or *kriss,* dispatching everybody in sight. Eventually, the Dutch captain had put an end to him with a well-aimed shot. I gathered from Mr Maconochie that in fact it wasn't exactly an everyday occurrence, and that I had been a bit unlucky to have run into it so early in my career. He pointed out that perhaps, on the other hand, I'd been fortunate in not arriving just a few moments earlier, when I too might have become a corpse. I hadn't thought of that aspect.

Invited to dinner with Mr and Mrs Maconochie, this

cheerful Scot with a happy laugh told me that he'd been perpetually 'broke' because for years he'd been paying off a breach-of-promise injunction. Mrs Maconochie looked slightly sour at this disclosure. He was evidently a good businessman and was highly popular with the Chinese.

However, only a few months after my arrival he suddenly vanished from our scene, and I saw him no more. I tried to find out where he had gone, but the only response was fingers to the lips and an insistent 'shush'. His place was taken by another fine manager by the name of George Lewis, who had been decorated in the War, clearly a *Tuan Besar* in the making.

One of the few accolades of my life in commerce came from Lewis; he gave me good marks for promoting the sales of somebody or other's biscuits for which we were agents.

By then I was out on my own in the markets, and no longer a pupil of Swee Leong. Gaining rapidly in confidence and experience, I was getting well known in downtown Singapore.

I loved the whole atmosphere – the excruciating smells, the jangling Chinese music and the people with whom I had to rub shoulders. In particular I found the *towkays* most pleasant to deal with, and I became acquainted with some of the families, which seemed to be legion. I fear that our office reckoning wasn't always in accord with my own over goods sold on credit, and I was admonished several times when a *towkay 'jattoed'* (went bankrupt) and couldn't pay what he owed us. This *jatto* sometimes caused consternation, as in the case of Bun Bee, a very well-known grocer in Market Street. He was charm itself, spoke perfect English, and was beloved by the European *Mem-Tuans* (white goddesses).

And then he went and *jattoed.* Shockwaves went through the entire Colony and the mercantile houses including my own company, lost a lot of money. I had cheerfully executed orders from him without a thought of disaster; indeed, none of our people had a hint of trouble, and even the omniscient Hoo Teck was completely taken aback. Just before the news broke, the wily Bun Hee had sailed for China.

However, I do remember one item on the credit side of my activities. Louis Barron, the head of Carreras in London, had decided to make the 'perfect' cigarette. So my company, agents for Carreras, bought up a number of cases of the new White Eagle cigarettes, hoping to make a bomb. In fact, they were too expensive and too pure altogether, and didn't sell.

But one day in downtown Singapore, a taxi driven by a Bengali swerved round a corner. I just managed to push a Chinese child out of the way, getting scraped myself. There was the usual altercation, and when I left, the Bengali was still being beaten to a pulp.

Somebody tracked me down, and I was invited to a feast at the house of a wealthy Chinese, who was evidently the child's grandfather. He couldn't speak English or Malay, but a member of the household did the interpreting with an Oxbridge accent. The talk ran on trade, on which I now considered myself an expert. I recounted the Louis Barron experiment that had backfired, and produced my cigarette case, full of White Eagles. The old grandfather took one, smoked it, looked thoughtful and then said he would buy our entire stock. I hoped for a small bonus from the company, but no joy – just a pleasant word from George Lewis.

Many of the Malayan Chinese community were known as 'Straits' Chinese, which meant that they were from families that had been domiciled in the country for several generations. There were, of course, many others, who were relatively new immigrants from various parts of China.

At Chinese New Year, people like me, who spent their time out and around the markets, were expected to go and drink with the *towkays.* One had to do the rounds, and the drinks mixture was lethal. There were means of emerging from this ordeal fairly unscathed, if one knew how to go about it, but during this first year I came badly to grief, and I believe that the last *towkay* I had been able to visit had to have me poured into a taxi and taken home. This was in the days when I was still doing the boarding-house round, and I was told later by my very understanding landlady that she had met me crawling on all fours up the stairs. I was arrayed in an Egyptian-style Fez cap and a false pigtail, and my pockets were bulging with an assortment of cigars presented to me by the *towkays.* One was always excused going to the office on the day following Chinese New Year.

Singapore lies only very minimally above the equator and the climate is very sticky, so one sweltered and sweated most of the time. Accordingly one needed around a dozen suits of white 'ducks', which on first arrival were run up at minimal cost almost overnight by Chinese tailors.

Often you needed to change at midday; in those days air-conditioning was unheard of. I feel sure too that even the Frigidaire hadn't yet been invented – food and drinks were kept cool by enormous blocks of ice that would be brought from somewhere by one of the domestics, either on his bicycle, tied to the crossbar, or else in a rickshaw.

A dress variation was the *tutup* (closed), which was a jacket buttoned up to the neck. This was peculiar to the Singapore brokers who worked in a small lane very close to our own offices known as 'Shark's Alley'.

As for sanitary arrangements – words fail me. I loathed them. Only at the Cricket Club and at the hotels was there any decent sanitation, which was reason enough for me to start spending more time at the former.

3

'Riff Raff'

Malaya and Singapore were fervent in their membership of that great Empire upon which the sun was expected to shine for ever.

I doubt whether anyone in that steaming cauldron of enterprise and hedonism ever dreamed that it could be otherwise. Indeed, a decade after me, the lights still shone on the dancing, wining, dining multitude as the Japanese took up their menacing station on the other side of the causeway from the mainland.

India was of course the Crown Jewel of the Empire, superior in every respect to all other imperial possessions, but the Malaya Civil Service (MCS) considered that it was a very good second. I have, none the less, heard some lively disputes concerning the rival claims of Ceylon and the Sudan.

The Indian model was closely followed wherever it could be applied, and there was indeed an unwritten code of conduct that had to be learnt very quickly, rather like going to school again.

The *Mem-Tuans* were the school prefects who would do their best to indoctrinate all new young men. Looking back, I recall some remarkable women who were a cross between Trollope's Mrs Proudie and Kipling's Mrs Hawsbee.

One of the chief social curses of those days was the calling card. You had to have a large number of white cards with your name engraved, not printed, on them. Armed with a list of important people, you got into a rickshaw and toured the local equivalent of Hampstead, where all these exalted ones lived.

Outside their 'residences' (they didn't live like normal people in houses or bungalows) there would be a box with a slot in it. If there was a notice saying 'Not at Home', you would drop through the slot not one card but two; this was very important.

I can't remember the procedure if your prey was 'At Home'; I don't think I bothered much about this distinction. I just rammed my cards through the slot and fled. Thus you did your social duty and, unless you put up a terrible black at the club, or offended one of the wives, you became acceptable. However, you did not find an automatic place in the social diary.

So far as I remember, none of my calls were returned.

If you belonged to one of the 'pukka' companies, your call would be acknowledged by a card from the appropriate nabob, which would be posted on the notice board in the Cricket Club, which all young men were expected to join. this might – particularly if you were a Blue – be followed by an invitation to dinner. Mercifully I myself was spared most of these miseries, but I was collared early on for a *pahit* (drinks) party at which, hopelessly out my depth, I didn't distinguish myself and was never asked again.

And then, of course, there was what is nowadays known as the 'Colour Bar' – and a very real thing it was too. I expect most of the Whites believed – as I did – that colour is really quite irrelevant, but here and there in this world one encounters groups of people with whom – quite regardless of their colour – one's feelings are adrift, while with others there is a natural affinity. Speaking for myself, I have always reserved the right to like or dislike people in accordance with that strange phenomenon called 'wavelength', but colour has never been a criterion. However, in those Imperial days there wasn't very much social mixing in the clubs and hotels. Singapore did have one multi-racial tennis club, but that was all; and if a young man wanted to associate with a girl of 'different' blood, he had to be careful about where he went and who might see him.

I recall that all this social nonsense used to cause much amusement among the Chinese. I suppose the time-scale of Chinese civilization puts them at an advantage and gives them a kind of superiority complex. They certainly found much amusement in the strange attitudes and goings-on of the Europeans in their midst.

Still, an Englishman's club is very much part of his culture, especially when he's away from home. To us, the club is a place where we can meet with people of similar background and exchange confidences and ideas.

With cricket, it has always been different. The slave in the West Indies played happily with his master, and on the turf they found rare equality. The need of the master for good native players, and the opportunity which those players found to achieve some sort of dignity under abject conditions, must surely account for the unique place of cricket in those Caribbean countries' make-up, now and in the past. The game is a great leveller, and in Malaya sheer merit ensured places in representative teams for Eurasians, Chinese and Indians – however, come to think of it, I don't recall any Malay cricketers.

I have already described how I arrived at the very purpose of our being, through my introduction to Sniffy Clark, and though there are people who think of cricketers a little differently and regard us as slightly mad, I swear that he who doesn't play the game – or doesn't at the very least score or umpire – lacks a social and philosophical arm that, in colonial days at any rate, was every bit as vital to his survival as the wing to a bird.

In Singapore, and indeed throughout Malaya, cricket was taken very seriously. It was rather like going back to school. If you possessed a resonant name that, through parentage or even the remotest kinship, rang through the cricket world, or even if you had simply achieved a mention in *Wisden* through having played for your school, then you could expect to go automatically into the top echelon without having to prove yourself. But if you were just an also-ran, you had to win your spurs at a lower level, where your cricket manners and indeed your entire personality would be closely scrutinized.

I have mentioned already the redoubtable Laverton, manager of Raffles and cricket maniac. Lavvy was the head of the junior cricket school, and if you wanted to play the game he would be prepared to give you a trial run, after a suitable introduction, of course, which in my case, as I have said, came from Sniffy Clark. But there were rules, and you had to learn them otherwise you were in for a jolt.

For instance, you were required to remember that on a certain day of the week between certain hours Lavvy would sit down in his office to arrange the lower level cricket schedules for the following weekend, and he didn't like it if you wasted his time by not being on the end of a telephone when he rang to ask you to play. Indeed, if you upset him by not being on hand, he might very well drop you from cricket for the following week, just to 'learn you'. You would normally be informed if you have incurred Lavvy's displeasure by his adjutant, who was called Bright, an employee of the Cable Company if I remember correctly.

Lavvy himself took much pride in a natural geniality, though there was betimes a steely glint in his eye, and so he exerted discipline through Bright, who didn't actually play but was always with us – umpiring, scoring and unfailingly drinking with us after a match.

Indeed, Bright was very necessary to our cricket well-being. Many years' acquaintance with the 'staff of life' (I refer to whisky rather than cricket in this context) had produced in Bright a deep, hoarse voice and a complexion that was almost mauve. He knew all the moves in cricket and was a stern disciplinarian.

It was Bright who gave us status by forming us into a Club called the 'Riff Raff' which had a Constitution and Rules and was highly exclusive. We even had a tie of such startling colours that those of us who had to wear it – and this was obligatory – felt somewhat abashed, particularly when we met a member of the upper cricket echelon. I distinctly remember, for instance, being scrutinized with well-bred dismay by Major Aeneas Quintus Perkins when I was wearing my tie in the early days of my membership of the club.

The standard of Riff Raff cricket was, I would say, of ordinary to middling club standard. We took it seriously, of course, particularly since Lavvy, who always kept wicket, would have it no other way; but not too seriously.

There were those among us who, like myself, had an eye on promotion to the upper echelon, but we all made the most of being Riff Raffs, and now and again there would be a 'non-cricket' Sunday, when a club outing was arranged by Bright.

I well remember the first such jaunt. We went on a picnic to a place in the Johore jungle called Kota Tinggi, where there was a waterfall. After gin and the picnic lunch, wearing nothing but swimming trunks, I climbed up the side of the waterfall, and there at the top I had my first view of Malay wildlife. Out of the jungle, loping obliquely across my front, was a glorious black panther. It saw me but looked bored, and after a drink from the rivulet it was crossing, it continued on its way, its long tail waving to and fro.

It was around this time that I put up a bit of a cricket 'black', playing for the Riff Raff.

We just couldn't dismiss our opponents' last batsman; he blocked everything and was clearly bent on playing out time. I was put on to bowl by Lavvy, and after a couple of unproductive overs I had a brainwave. I tossed the ball up so high that it came down straight on top of the stumps. The immovable batsman stepped back on his wicket – just as I hoped he would – and we won the match. It wasn't the first time a bowler had used that trick, of course, but on that occasion it was regarded by many on both sides as unfair, indeed as a bit of a cad's trick. I slunk away disconsolate, fearing that the affair would affect my promotion ambitions. I needn't have worried. When the all-powerful Sniffy heard about it he smiled and said, 'Not quite cricket, and not quite original either.'

His was, as always, the last word.

There was another occasion when we came badly to grief. We were playing a Chinese XI, and one of their number was a diminutive ever-smiling schoolboy of about 16 or 17, called Ping.

We went in first, but in due course Ping started to bowl. He only took four or five steps, but in shocked surprise we found we were up against a fast bowler of no ordinary pace. Indeed he slung the ball down with astonishing velocity, and we lost wickets quickly. Not to put too fine a point on it, Ping went straight through us. There was no question of his bowling short or what were to become known as bouncers on the West Indian model; he kept them on a good length, and for most of us he was just too fast. Inevitably, he inflicted casualties in his triumphant progress.

Pavilion dressing rooms around Singapore became littered with dented 'boxes' as a result of Ping's efforts. He did seem to inflict damage with uncanny accuracy on that portion of the male anatomy most vulnerable to the fast rising ball. As a result, a new word was coined on those Far Eastern cricket fields – 'pinged'. I myself was badly pinged by the master on another occasion, playing in a representative fixture.

One of our top Singapore cricketers had played against the express Australian pair Gregory and McDonald and he believed that Ping as he matured was the quickest bowler he'd ever faced. Ping was later to play with the representatve Malaya side in a triangular 'Test' series with Hong Kong and Shanghai. I believe he won the Hong Kong match for Malaya, but I heard that the class Shanghai batsmen managed to get the better of him.

The governing body of Singapore Cricket was known colloquially, and rather irreverently, as the 'Holy Synod'. Its President, of whom, I have already had much to say, Sniffy Clark, was our chief of men, mostly *in absentia.* He was a busy man not much given to committee deliberations. In other words, he didn't like constraints. But his name and occasional presence gave tone and Government backing to the Synod.

In the absence of the President, the Committee was normally chaired by the formidable 'A.K.' It used to gather on most evenings on the lower verandah of the Singapore Cricket Club's pavilion. Its members were mostly well-known names in the cricket world, and they were always addressed (provided there had been suitable introductions) by their initials, nicknames or first names.

Of A.K. himself, stories were legion, but nobody ever used his name, and it was many a year before I found out what it was, though I believe even that may have been assumed; let's say it was *Hetherington.* In World War One he was said to have gone 'over the top' waving a cricket bat and shouting, 'Come on lads, get at 'em' and somehow surviving the lethal response of the massed German machine guns.

A.K. was said to have played first-class cricket before going East, and he was very pukka indeed. He made all the right noises and belonged to all the right clubs in Britain, while in Singapore the *Tuan Besars* and their *Mems* were glad to know him and to defer to him.

The Committee, apart from A.K., consisted of R.N. Hamilton (R.N.), R.L. Braddell (Bobby), G.E. Livock (Gerry), D.V. Hill (Hookey), G.L. Bryan (Godfrey), D.L.A. Hoblyn (Donald), P.H. Stewart-Brown (S.B.); now and again others would be brought in for consultation.

Hill had only just missed playing for England. I suspect his moment had come and gone, however, and his venom as a fast bowler had declined in the heat of Singapore. Braddell was getting a bit past it, too. He had been given his Blue just before the war.

The youngest of the Synod was Philip Stewart-Brown, a Harrovian and Oxford Blue who had been the best schoolboy cricketer of his year, and had played some fine innings at top level. Unfortunately, he never seemed to do very well in Singapore.

I heard later from a friend of Lavvy's something of the typical dialogue of a Synod meeting. Lavvy had been summoned to attend.

A.K.: 'Good evening, Laverton. Have a drink. We were wondering how those colts of yours are coming along. Any useful prospects?'

Lavvy: 'Yes A.K., I think we have one or two possibilities. Young Begley's a good bowling prospect. Pretty fast and seams them both ways. I think you'll find he's the right sort, and should be an asset. Imray has cricket in him, but he needs knocking into shape; you might perhaps give him a go.'

A.K.: 'Thank you, Laverton. I see you've finished your drink. I think that will be all. Agreed, R.N.?'

Hamilton nods agreement and Lavvy departs.

Not long after the meeting to which this report referred, my great moment arrived. Signalled by Hoblyn, who was doing duty as ADC to A.K., I approached the sacred table, bowed to A.K. and said, 'Good evening, sir.'

A.K.: 'A.K. will do, my boy. Have a drink; we wanted a word with you. Mr Clark speaks well of you, and your captain Laverton seems pleased and thinks we should give you a trial in the next representative game. We've decided to include you and Begley in the Merchants' XI to play against Public Services and Law. Donald here will skipper the Merchants, and Bobby the PS and L. Eh, Bobby?'

So there it was. I acquitted myself reasonably well, behaved evidently with the required decorum, and held two good catches. I had entered Singapore's cricket society.

I soon had trouble with Major Aeneas Quintus Perkins. I always seemed to rub him up the wrong way on the cricket field. I just couldn't bring myself to call this taciturn, beetle-browed, fiercely moustached officer by his name – Aeneas. He could strike you down with one of his fierce looks. Come to think of it, I doubt whether I ever heard him utter a word until the day when, taking a short run off his bowling, I just got home, ran past the crease, tripped over his foot, and heard him give vent very distinctly to a four-letter word.

Normally he would converse by means of one explosive sound 'Hah'. How he ever managed to get through public school and Sandhurst (or maybe 'The Shop') with a name like Aeneas I just can't imagine.

Yet he was evidently quite a man in his own right; I heard he'd had a pretty impressive war. Anyway, the young officers of the garrison were scared stiff of him. I knew quite a lot of regimental tittle-tattle through my friend Roger Welchman, a subaltern who oddly enough, considering his name, belonged to the Welch Regiment, which had recently arrived from India.

Until around 4 p.m., when the sun was considered to have lost its power, men on the field would normally wear the wide-brimmed 'double *terai*' felt hat. After that hour there would be a blossoming and one would see an array of well-known club caps, and it became clear that the world of cricket was very well represented in Singapore.

Indeed, Malay cricketers were still bubbling at this time, having defeated a touring Australian XI several years earlier, Admittedly the Australians would probably have regarded their one-day Malayan fixture as a piece of holiday recreation; however, their team did include some of the great ones like Macartney, Woodfull, Ponsford, and so on. I've never been able to see the score card, which must have been interesting.

The Malayan captain had been J.H.N. (Johnnie) Foster, the youngest of the seven Foster brothers of Malvern and Worcestershire. The eldest, R.E., was to play famously for England against Australia and to make a score that stood as an individual record until Donald Bradman came along.

Johnnie was still in Malaya in my time, rubber planting somewhere up in the FMS backblocks. Anyway, in this match against the Australians Malaya had made a respectable score, thanks to a fine century by a young man called Brooks.

All the same, the Australians looked set to win easily until a whispered conference between Johnnie and the star bowler, Doctor John Hennessey, changed things dramatically.

'What are we going to do about Woodfull?'

A field-placing plot was hatched, and Woodfull fell for it; I believe he was caught somewhere in a leg trap; and thereafter Hennessey went through the Australian side.

I've heard the story a dozen times from Johnnie himself when, years later, I used to meet him on the Hove County ground. It – the story – used to take him half an hour or so.

An interesting aspect of cricket as a game is the demands it makes on character. It has always been my experience that the higher up the ladder you go the better you tend to play. Certainly my own performances at the higher level were far better than they had been with the Riff Raffs under Lavvy, much though I enjoyed playing in that remarkable side.

I remained a Riff Raff throughout my stay in Singapore and Malaya, but I became a rather elevated one. Periodically, if not required for one of the many representative games that punctuated the Malay season, I would return to play under Lavvy.

I was selected on several occasions by the Synod to play for Singapore against sides such as FMS, the Civil Service and Combined Services. But one year there came a serious hitch.

The annual three-day Colony v FMS match was coming up. I mightn't have been selected, of course, but in any case the fixture had to be postponed because the date clashed with a full-scale military exercise that was to last for two days and had to take precedence even over cricket.

I had by then joined the SVC (Singapore Volunteer Corps) – a motley defence body which consisted of six companies 'A' Machine Gun Company, 'B' Eurasian, 'C' Scottish (heavily over-subscribed), 'D' Indian, 'E' Chinese and 'F' Malay. There was, in addition, an HQ Company. All able-bodied Europeans were expected to join. I was with A Company.

A.K. held senior rank at Corps Headquarters. The whole thing was taken very seriously. The regular garrison in those days consisted of the 2nd Battalion the Welch Regiment; the

Gunners and the Engineers were on the nearby islands of Blachan Mati and Pulau Brani respectively.

The plan for this exercise was that we would all be conveyed by cruiser to a point out at sea, when we would go ashore in boats, neutralize a mythical opposition on the beaches and then move inland and capture Singapore. The whole performance was to be based on the element of silent surprise. Any man found talking would be hanged, drawn and quartered. It was just like a re-enactment of the 1915 holocaust under Sir Ian Hamilton at Gallipoli, except that there were to be no Turks to mow us down. Like most military exercises, it was all wildly uncomfortable and not very convincing.

However, I might well have been the sole fatal casualty. Having got ashore, we were moving inland to silence the heavy guns, which should in theory neutralize any landings from the sea.

We had to make our way through some thick scrub, and we were commanded in this our first attack wave by none other than Major Aeneas Quintus Perkins, with A.K. as his second in command. I have often wondered how the two of them got along. A.K. was once heard to say, 'Never can get much out of the feller.'

But there we were very much on our mettle, advancing in extended order through the scrub, and suddenly a snake reared up and bit me on the leg. Somewhere during my spasmodic and thoroughly inglorious military career, from the Malvern OTC onwards, I was equipped with brown leather gaiters. I can't recall whether I was wearing these during this particular exercise or whether I simply had thick puttees. Anyway, expecting at any moment to drop dead, I struggled on and finished the exercise still alive.

We went into camp for the night. Again, it was very uncomfortable indeed, as I suppose it was meant to be. On the following morning we were addressed by the GOC. He talked about Singapore's impregnable defences and about how its enormous guns would decimate any attempted landing from the sea. The General declared himself well satisfied and congratulated us on having taken the defences completely by surprise.

I had been pondering upon all this, and when we were asked if we had any questions and after all the important people had had their say, I rose trembling to my feet.

'Sir,' I quavered (and I could see Aeneas Quintus eyeing me), 'what would happen should an enemy decide to attack from the FMS across the Causeway?'

There was a dreadful silence, then – 'When you have been in this country a little longer, young man, you will realize that not only have we excellent defences right through the peninsular, but that any attack through the jungle is unthinkable; it is just not possible.'

So there it was. I was elsewhere when the Japanese attacked, but I remember thinking on those words.

There came an unhappy day when we lost Lavvy. He and his bosses at the Raffles Hotel fell out over some matter or other that was later described as 'trivial'. Anyway, this was the end of Lavvy in Singapore, and all that we Riff Raffs could do was to wish him 'God speed' over a few drinks in the ship's bar just before he sailed to take up his next appointment.

As we said our farewells and went ashore, Bright showed his real form. He deployed us in two ranks down at the quayside and briefed us on what we had to do.

'As the ship starts to move, I shall call "Riff Raffs, attenshun", but mind, I shall be the only one that salutes.'

And so it was. As the anchor was raised and the ship slowly left the dock, we all stood rigidly to attention while Bright stood with his hand raised to his solar topee in salute; and Lavvy, clearly visible at the ship's rail, waved regally in acknowledgement. Bright's past as an RSM – or was it CSM? – stood him in good stead. It was all very sad. I began to feel that my new world was collapsing. First Maconochie and now Lavvy. What next?

Well, there came a Mess night with the Welch Regiment, at which I was the only 'guest'. In those days, other garrison personnel were eligible for honorary membership of regimental messes, and several of my friends and associates were there as of right – including Bryan, Hill, Livock and virtually all members of the Synod. I was a guest of my friend Roger Welchman.

He hadn't told me of the Mess tradition that nobody might leave the table at the end of dinner until, following the port, the senior guest made a move. As it happened on this particular evening, I was the only guest, and this was the first time that I had dined in a military Mess.

It was a most intimidating experience, particularly for a fledgling. There were the lights, the officers in Mess kit, the soldier servants, the regimental silver, the bugler, and the air of well-bred decorum. And, to cap it all, as the guest for the evening I was planted immediately on the Colonel's right.

I was frankly scared stiff to begin with, though as dinner proceeded I became more mellow, very conscious however that I must be on my guard against a 'black'.

By the time the port had been round thrice I was at my ease, surrounded by a pleasant haze and becoming talkative. I had commenced giving the Colonel the benefit of my wisdom and experience when I caught the eye of Aeneas Q. Perkins at the other end of the table. He was being regaled by a chatty captain, but I noted that he was observing me and had started to twirl his moustache, which with Aeneas meant silent disapproval. I noted too that Godfrey Bryan, the picture of resignation, was sitting there looking down at his port glass.

Eventually, Roger whispered to me that I must make a move. Horrified, I caught the Colonel's eye and, half-rising, he said, 'Shall we make a move?' And so we did, and the tension lifted. As we strolled into the ante-room, the Colonel took Perkins by the arm and said, 'Aeneas, I'd like a word with you.'

They vanished, and that was the last I ever saw of that astonishing man. I suppose he was posted elsewhere. Perhaps a secret assignment of sorts. He may not have added lustre to our conversations, but by his departure Singapore lost a very fair spin bowler and a useful No. 6 batsman.

4

Cigarettes and Whisky

Mr Hill, F.J., our Singapore director, was a handsome man. Come to think of it, he was probably the most handsome man I had ever encountered - as well as the most astute.

'It's time you had a short break from Singapore,' he said to me. 'I'm sending you up to Kota Bahru in Kelantan with Morris.' Gerald Morris had taken over from Heath as our cigarette purveyor.

'I want you to watch him at work,' he went on, 'and so I'm giving you a chit to Aubrey Wallich, who is Boustead's agent in Kelantan. He'll look after you.'

This was splendid news for me. Kelantan in those days was as remote as Outer Mongolia, and I was agog to see it.

At the Cricket Club I ran into A.K. and told him of my good fortune.

'Ah, Wallich,' he said, 'yes, fine feller. I'll give you a chit to him.' So now I had two chits to Wallich, and wondered whether this might be overdoing it a bit.

Morris and I sailed one afternoon on a coastal steamer bound for Bangkok. It would deposit us at Tumpat, the port for Kota Bahru. At dinner that evening, the Captain told us a story of something that had happened only about 18 months previously.

As well as I can remember it, the saga was thus:

We are sometimes commissioned to take bullion

> up to Hong Kong, and so it was on this particular occasion. We had, as always, a bullion guard supplied by the Singapore Volunteer Corps, and there was as usual an armed guard on duty at the hatch where the bullion was placed. I remember that we had embarked at Singapore a number of Chinese priests. It was dark, and we were hugging the coast as near as possible as there were storms out at sea. We had just about got opposite Bias Bay when I found suddenly that I was locked in my cabin, and at the same time I realized that the engines had stopped. There was no way I could get out. I rang the Chief Officer and the Chief Engineer. There was no answer from one, and the other was also locked in his cabin. The upshot, as we pieced together later, was that our missionary clergy were pirates. They had immobilized our officers and crew, also the off-duty members of the bullion guard who, as it happened, were living it up in the Saloon in which they also were locked up. They overpowered the sentry and did the same to the Chief Engineer, who was compelled to stop the engines. They then transferred the bullion to a junk that had come out from the shore and was alongside us. In due course, somebody broke free and released us, but the pirates and the bullion were of course well away . . .

An absorbing story, if told with a touch of license. But I was assured it was substantially true. The sequel, as we heard later, was that no longer was the SVC asked to supply a bullion guard when it was needed. This duty was henceforth performed by regular soldiers from the garrison.

I can't recall what Tumpat looked like when we reached it next morning. It may have been palm-fringed, or it may have been nestling among those cursed mangroves that I was to learn later in my career to loathe exceedingly.

Anyway, we were decanted by basket into a barge of some sort and then conveyed up river to Kota Bahru, a mile or so away. And there on the quayside was a florid man of medium height, wearing a monocle. It was Aubrey Wallich, who at once began to talk in a most persuasive manner.

We were to stay at the Rest House, Aubrey told us, as he hadn't much room in his house, but we were to dine with him that night. I was a Malvernian, so he'd heard, and so, of course, I played cricket. He, too, had been at Malvern. Here he took a deep breath and then told us that he was arranging a cricket match and he'd tell us about it later.

Did Gerald Morris play cricket?

No he didn't, and he couldn't tell one end of a bat from the other. Never mind, he'd learn. We would have to teach him the basics, he said, since he needed every man he could get for the forthcoming match.

All this came pouring out of Aubrey in the first few minutes. He was very talkative and very persuasive; there was a certain aura about him. I was moreover reminded of something our captain had said the night before at dinner:

'Going to meet Aubrey Wallich, are you? Don't be misled. You may think he's all froth and bubble, but he's not; he's one of the shrewdest customers I've ever met and that's going some. And he always manages to get his way.'

Gerald did manage to splutter that he'd come up to Kelantan to sell cigarettes, but Aubrey said yes, he'd arranged all that and Gerald would be able to sell cases and cases of cigarettes, but that cricket was on his mind at that moment.

One had the feeling that there were strictly ordered priorities in Kelantan.

Gerald, fortunately, had a splendid sense of humour. However, at the Rest House, a huge wooden bat-infested structure, he did evince some anxiety: 'I do hope Aubrey's arrangements are with the right agents and for the right brands of cigarettes. I hope he knows that I represent Carreras and not BAT.'

We had noticed a very handsome Malay girl in native dress hanging around the Rest House entrance. Suddenly, in marched a square dark-featured man dressed in a jungle outfit. Into a room he went, followed by the Malay girl, and he may well have remained there for the next two days. We never saw him in the dining room, and all we knew of his presence was that periodically he shouted for coffee through a half-open door.

Aubrey was a bachelor, as we already knew, and that evening at his house it was clear that he did himself very well indeed. Asked about the man at the Rest House he came out with a customary torrent of biographical detail: 'Oh yes, that's Mike Moran. He spends most of his time prospecting way out in the jungle, and then comes in here for a few days' rest. The girl's name is Halowe, and she's been with him for quite a while. A silent man, Mike, but a good feller. Good war record. Matter of fact, he spent several years in the French Foreign Legion; ran away from school in order to join. Got mixed up in that affair at Ain Agoula down in the Sahara.'

I discovered later that Mike was one of the few survivors among 50 men when a Legion fort was attacked. They were rescued in the nick of time.

Aubrey was the perfect host at dinner. When the subject of A.K. arose, his bubbling discourse became more restrained and more thoughtful. He obviously had a very high regard for A.K., and we pressed him to tell us more.

'You'd think he was an aristocrat from his manner, but he's not. Comes from a very ordinary family background. My father and his knew each other. However, A.K. does anything he wants to do much better than any man I know. For one thing he's a quite brilliant linguist. Seems to be a natural, and picks up dialects in no time at all. Of course he's a wealthy man, but there's no question of his having inherited; he's done it all himself speculating on the Stock Exchange. Told me once how he did it. He's a born leader.'

He went on apace.

'You know Sniffy Clark, of course?' I nodded. 'Well, Sniffy knows A.K. better than most and probably knows something of his activities; A.K. himself is very adroit at parrying questions, but I'm pretty sure he has some connection with the FO. Of course, we've all got our Achilles heel, and A.K. likes the ladies rather more than is good for him. And they like him too. Result is that there are some irate husbands around. A.K. vanishes every now and then, you know, ostensibly on bird-watching trips, the feathered variety, of course. But I believe he gets up the China coast quite a bit, and over to Java and Sumatra. This is all very hush-hush, but I believe he takes on a new identity. In fact, I've an idea he has several different names according to where he is and what's he's doing, but that's another matter.' [Long pause] 'Something to do with Intelligence, I shouldn't wonder. It was only about eighteen months ago that he got mixed up in that big show in Shanghai. They say he was some kind of liaison officer with the Shanghai Defence Force. Dam' lucky to get out alive, from all accounts. He's very caustic about the in-fighting that goes on in Whitehall. Says the FO never really knows what it's doing on Eastern matters, but that the India Office has its feet on the ground.'

There was another unexpected pause.

Then, 'Enough of A.K. . . . I want to get these people (the locals) interested in sport, especially cricket. You know, something of the spirit of the game. The District Officer's no good in that regard. Decent enough fellow, but he's always away from base. Sniffy reckons the trouble is he's not a cricketer.'

Aubrey warmed to his theme and Gerald, who was Jewish, found it hard to contain his amusement.

We learnt that an actual match threatened. It was to be on Saturday – it was now Tuesday – between Kota Bahru and The Gentlemen of the Ulu (Jungle). It was to be played near a place called Kuala Krai, about 20 or 30 miles from Kota

Bahru, because this would be more suitable for the Ulus, who would be mainly rubber planters, prospectors and tin miners. It was clear that Aubrey had everything in hand. If I had time he would run me out before the big day, as he wanted to make sure that the ground was in order.

Gerald and I felt quite exhausted, when we returned to the Rest House. Aubrey was a great host, but his exuberance had the effect of draining one of energy.

During the next couple of days we went about our business with the Kota Bahru *towkays* and Indian traders, and Gerald, despite his earlier misgivings, did some good business; indeed, his path had been well prepared by Aubrey.

Then Aubrey and I had our 'run out' to Kuala Krai. This entailed bouncing and grinding along a very rough jungle track in Aubrey's specially reinforced vehicle.

Eventually we came to a saucer-shaped hollow surrounded by virgin jungle that was being worked on by a posse of prisoners from the Kota Bahru gaol. Every now and then one of the guards would fire a shot from his rifle in order to scare off any wild animals that might be around. All kinds of creatures were said to live in these jungles.

Some of the prisoners were at work digging out tree stumps; others were disconsolately dragging a mat backwards and forwards along a flattish piece in the middle at the bottom of the saucer. This was to do duty as the pitch, and Aubrey said it would be all right on the day.

It was now Friday, and the match was to be on the morrow. I felt a little dubious, but who was I to express an opinion? How did Aubrey manage to communicate with these remote Ulus, I wanted to know, as the telephone system, where it existed, was very rudimentary. 'Oh, that's quite easy,' said Aubrey, 'we do it by runner.'

Saturday morning dawned, and it was raining. At breakfast Gerald said, 'Oh God, poor Aubrey. I do hope it clears.' Eventually, the rain did stop, and when we repaired to Aubrey, there he was with all the gear and an umbrella, looking anxiously at the skies.

'Looks like a sticky wicket,' he said. 'Can't make up my mind what to do if I win the toss.' He had hired a van to convey the Kota Bahrus, and we were introduced to Aubrey's henchman, a European foreman of the Public Works Department who was also at that time warden of the local gaol.

Our team included a couple of Indians, two Chinese – one of them a big fat *towkay* – a Dutch sailor who had been left behind by his ship while in a drunken stupor, Aubrey's Goanese clerk to umpire at one end and a senior schoolgirl to do likewise at the other. There was another schoolgirl to do the scoring. At his wits' end to complete the XI, Aubrey had brought in a prison warder and a 'good' prisoner. The arrival of Gerald and myself had been a godsend. Another prisoner, categorized as 'semi-good', whom Aubrey had been coaching, would be 12th man.

We left in convoy with Aubrey, Gerald and I, plus the gear in Aubrey's vehicle. We slithered and slid along the track and eventually arrived safe and sound at Krai.

The rain had kept off.

The Ulus, less Mike Moran who was to captain the side, were all assembled – which says much for Aubrey's 'runner' system – and they were just as motley a lot as the rest of us. Few of them knew anything about cricket, and if they had known anything once, they'd forgotten it.

Aubrey was the only one on either side who was properly attired in whites, and there he was wearing his English club blazer and cap.

'Where's Moran?' asked Aubrey. Nobody seemed to know, and we had to start without him. Aubrey won the toss and decided to bat. 'Tricky decision to have to make,' he said.

He and I opened the innings and had already made quite a few runs on this very 'dodgy' wicket of Aubrey's, against bowling that – to say the least – lacked practice.

Then Moran arrived, late but unapologetic.

He started to bowl, and the picture changed abruptly. On that unpredictable wicket his fast bowling was lethal. I was soon bowled neck and crop, and Aubrey received one in a tender place and had to be helped to the sidelines, where Halowe, who had arrived with Moran, was 'helping' the Chinese schoolgirl do the scoring.

Under Moran's ruthless attack we Kota Bahrus wilted and collapsed, and the Ulus took new heart. Only a tail-end Indian in our line-up offered any further resistance. With bat flailing like a scythe, he somehow connected time and again and amassed 20 or so valuable runs, surviving two obvious run-outs when the schoolgirl umpire was looking the other way and conducting a sign-language conversation with her girl friend with the score sheet.

Aubrey wasn't the only casualty. Moran himself fell over in surprise and pummelled the ground as if in a fit after our lady umpire – put up to it by one of the close fielders – screamed in her high-pitched girlish voice 'Nar baall!' raising her right arm, as she had been instructed. But the demon bowler recovered from the indignity and wrought yet more havoc.

The *towkay* got one in the mouth, and after we'd had at least one more 'retired hurt' the last two Kota Bahrus refused to face the massacre, and we ended the innings with some 80 runs for 8 wickets.

In the meantime the walking (or sitting) wounded had been joined by an Ulu who, fielding on the boundary, tripped over a tree stump, sat down heavily on some nasty spiked stuff, and was out of action.

Moran and a rubber planter who had once played for his school opened the Ulu batting, and I was deputed to bowl. The 'good' prisoner who, coached by Aubrey in the prison yard, had shown some aptitude, was to bowl at the other end. Aubrey, perforce, was still nursing his injury on the sideline.

Moran had clearly batted before. For a couple of overs he played carefully, though nearly bowled by the 'good' prisoner from one that shot along the ground after hitting a bump. The 'good' prisoner's bowling action – be it noted – looked suspiciously like a throw.

Then Moran once again started to show his mettle. Leaping down the pitch to ball after ball, he let fly with straight and cover drives for four and six, deft flicks to fine leg, smashes to midwicket and deep square and just about all other points of the compass. We could do nothing with him.

Once, when he stood at the bowler's end and I waited for the ball to be thrown at me, Moran rubbed salt in the wound by asking me if I had any special reason for bowling to him without an extra cover. In fact, Gerald had reorganized the field in a moment of panic and left me naked, as it were.

There was one occasion when he might have been out. He skied one off my bowling and Gerald, fielding on the boundary at jungle-edge midwicket, judged it perfectly, but he was off-balance and his outstretched hands were not quite in the right place. The ball hit him on the shoulder, and he too had to retire.

Then our keeper, the Dutch sailor, became difficult. Moran had stepped way out of crease and missed the ball, but our keeper failed to stump him. Here was a gift run-out, with Moran yards out of his crease, but the Dutchman just stood there and stared. Not to put too fine a point on it, he had no idea what to do as the ball was returned to him hard and low, and the lucky Moran was at least two yards from home.

Jim, the Foreman of Works, shouted, 'You stupid bastard.' With that the Dutchman cursed in his native tongue and kicked down the stumps. Aubrey was not amused.

However, we settled down to it again, but spent much time searching for the ball, dispatched into the jungle by Moran, who by now had his eye in and was having a field day.

Inevitably there came a time when we couldn't find the ball and reluctantly Aubrey produced his spare. When, shortly afterwards, that one was lost too, Aubrey saw his opportunity to save face. The opposition were two short of the modest target we had set without loss, but he pointed out that he'd started the match with two balls but both had been lost in the rough, and clearly the match could not be completed. It would have to end in a draw.

I remember that when we were searching for the second ball Moran said, chattily, 'Look, paw marks; a tigress and her cub, and fresh too.'

There was in fact a certain altercation about who had really won – despite Aubrey's settling for a draw. The Ulus said that with Moran in full blast, the result was a foregone conclusion, but Aubrey insisted that the laws of cricket are the laws of cricket, and there the matter ended.

We were not quite finished, however.

As we were de-bussing at Kota Bahru, the Dutchman who had evidently been brooding, said to Jim the Foreman, 'You call me bastard, eh? Take that.' And without more ado he landed a punch that would have done credit to 'Gentleman' Jackson. Our Jim collapsed like a house of cards. Aubrey, whom I had expected to treat the matter as a grave breach of discipline, to say nothing of cricket etiquette, said, 'Perhaps we'd better leave and let them get on with it.'

I do remember him saying a little later that he thought Sniffy's 'Cricket idea' was somewhat wasted on these fellers.'

I was to retain very happy memories of Kelantan and our inconclusive cricket match. I had been much amused by my first meeting with the ebullient Aubrey – I was not to know then that I would meet him again, in very different circumstances.

I ran into Ian Begley at the Singapore Cricket Club, following our return from Kelantan.

'Heard about Bright?' he asked.

I said I hadn't.

'Dead,' said Begley. 'Fell down in here with a heart attack just as he was drinking his first *stengah* of the evening.' Whisky and soda was always given its colloquial name at the club.

'And there's even worse. Remember Murdoch?'

I said I did. He was a Riff Raff, after all.

'Well,' said Begley, 'he's gone to prison for embezzling his

Company's funds. He always was a foose, of course.'

At that juncture A.K., who had arrived at the bar and was just ordering a drink, intervened. 'Forgive me, Begley, but just what is a foose?'

Begley hesitated, stammered a little, and before he could utter a coherent sentence, A.K. – always the essence of tact – said hastily, 'Forgive me, Begley. Of course I quite understand.'

I later learnt that foose was simply a bloody fool, and that it was Begley's own invention. Begley was entitled to kid-glove treatment at that stage. He had not yet achieved the status of being accorded his initials by the high priests of the Synod. For the moment he was just a junior ranker, known only by his surname to the likes of A.K. In due course he became I.B. In fact, Begley was commissioned on active service, as you might say.

He had had one of those cricket days when nothing could go wrong, and he had taken a number of good wickets very cheaply. Nobody could play him. As he walked off the field spectators in the pavilion rose to him, and A.K. shouted in a voice that all could hear, 'Well bowled, I.B.' Begley had come of age and joined the island's élite. A.K. then turned to me and asked about the Kelantan trip. 'Splendid fellow, A.W. I must get up there and see him. Excellent idea of his putting the prisoners through their paces; good thing if he could raise a prisoners' team; we might send the Riff Raffs to play them.'

I mentioned earlier the beautiful Dorothy in our company offices. I had some pleasant dealing with her, but I now learnt that she too was to leave us and go to England. It was understood that there had been some trouble with a parson, and her mother decided that Dorothy would be better away from Singapore for a while. I heard later that she took a job in our London office, where she disturbed everybody from the manager down to the office boy.

It had become a positive procession: Maconochie, Lavvy, Aeneas Perkins, Bright, Murdoch, and now Dorothy. And on top of all that, two members of the Synod went on long leave.

It was at about this juncture that I received my own marching orders. I was to become the company's cigarette purveyor throughout Johore and Malacca territory. I was to leave Singapore and base my activities on Malacca.

I immediately ran to Sniffy Clark, who seemed to have a roving commission throughout the territory south of Kuala Lumpur, to seek reassurance. I would be seeing much more of him in Malacca.

5

A New Role

I was soon to be given a new job, which involved cricket in an unexpected context. I was delighted at my good fortune. I was now to have an independent command, responsible only to F.J. in Singapore. I discovered that Hill was yet another Malvernian, senior however to Aubrey Wallich by some ten years.

And I was now to have a company car to enable me to travel. Since I couldn't drive, however, I was dependent for a while on a Malay chauffeur, or *syce* as they were called locally.

My first solo drive was inauspicious. It was in the streets of Malacca and mercifully I was crawling, but I hit a rickshaw, luckily without damaging the puller. There was no tiresome court case but the episode cost me some twenty Straits dollars, on top of the cost of having a new wheel put on the rickshaw. I was quick after that to learn the essential art of dodging the rickshaws, and there were no further costly mishaps.

Early on, I ran into A.L.B. Perkins, a fine cricketer who had also played rugby football for a top Welsh club. Hearing that he was a relative of Aeneas Quintus, I enquired. 'Believe it or not,' said Perkins, 'he's just got married, and is even learning to talk.' Our new Perkins was soon transferred to Singapore, and I learnt that he was early 'commissioned' and became known as A.L.B.

Many years later I ran into A.L.B. at the Nairobi Club in

Kenya, and asked again about Aeneas. 'Got a brood of about six,' said A.L.B., 'and they've all got Roman names. Something of the sort must run in the family. Anyway, Aeneas has again gone silent; the family was clearly just too much.'

Then came a keenly anticipated interview with Sniffy Clark, whom I always 'sir-d' because, after all, he was a very senior member of Government, and even though he was the head - senior even to A.K. - of the Synod in Singapore, where 'sir-ings' were taboo, it was clearly the right thing to pay him the respects that were then required from a young man to his seniors. Anyway, Sniffy called me to his Malacca office.

Sniffy was a big man in every way. Bulky of stature, good-looking, with greying hair and moustache, absolutely assured in manner, and utterly without 'side' or pretence.

His devotion to cricket verged on the eccentric, however. He saw the entire universe as a beautifully prepared greensward populated by figures in white, whose position in the scheme of things depended entirely on their ability with ball or bat.

'I've been talking to A.K. about you, and we think you're just the man we want to encourage cricket out there,' he said. 'Your company business will take you all over Malacca and Johore territory, and we think you should start a pilot scheme teaching the locals about cricket. You know, a bit of tuition and the cricket *Idea* - very important you know, the cricket Idea.' Muar - about 30 miles from Malacca - struck Sniffy as a good place to start.

'I've spoken to the DO (District Officer) - a good chap - forget his name - he'll help.'

He arranged for a cricket net and a mat with all necessary gear to be sent to Muar. 'We thought the space just outside the prison would be just about right for a ground,' he said. 'You'll no doubt be in Muar a lot, and you can occupy yourself doing a bit of coaching.'

He went on to say that A.W. (Aubrey Wallich) had come up with 'a good notion' about prisoners. 'We thought we'd start with them. After all, they've got to do as they are told, and then with luck we might expand outwards.'

The interview concluded on an expansive note. 'You know Scales, of course?'

I did, he was another Riff Raff. 'He's established in Muar now, and may be able to give you some help. If things go well we might be able to start up another cricket school down in Mersing – on the east coast of Johore. You'll be visiting there, I believe, and John Hinde (a rubber planter in Mersing) is an excellent fellow and dead keen on cricket. How d'you feel about it?'

I was, of course, honoured and delighted. I recall that it was during this conversation that Sniffy told me something about Aeneas Perkins that was interesting in this coaching connection:

'Aeneas was an excellent cricket coach,' said Sniffy.

'But sir,' I said, 'Major Perkins hardly ever opened his mouth.'

'No,' replied Sniffy, 'he didn't to you and to me, but he spoke to his troops, and he started a number of them playing cricket. There again, of course, like the prisoners, they had to do as they were told. But I feel sure we're on the right track with this sort of thing. Cricket is the key to so much that is worth while.'

Sniffy was of course a fanatic, but a very nice one, and I lapped up everything he said. Anyway, there it was, and whenever I could get to Muar, which was frequently, I had the wretched prisoners marched out and I chivvied them at the cricket net. Surprisingly, by the time I left Malacca some nine months later, I was able to report favourably to Sniffy, who on one or two occasions had come to inspect us at the nets. I think he was pleased as we had at least three promising prisoner colts and had even started to expand in order to include some trainees from Muar township itself, I think it fair to say, however, that during the course of our operations one of the prisoners ran away and was never heard of again.

Of course Sniffy exerted pressure; the matter was brushed

aside as an occupational hazard, and we carried on as usual. I sometimes wondered just how much of the cricket 'Idea' was sinking in with our colts. Down in Mersing, too, we managed to make a start. John Hinde was a great cricket fan, though not much of a performer, and his colts consisted of some of his Tamil rubber tappers plus his Chinese clerk.

Anyway, like Aubrey before us, we were making a start in bringing cricket to the backblocks of Empire, which – as Sniffy, A.K. and Aubrey all agreed – was the right and proper thing to do, and indeed as someone in the Synod once said: 'It's all part of the Splendour of our Heritage.' I wasn't entirely clear as to what this meant, but if one was in the cricket stream, one simply went along with all these things which came from on high. I did, of course, inform F.J. about my activities. His reply, 'What else would one expect of a Malvernian?', gave me the happy free hand that I needed.

I have to say in all honesty that Malacca cricket – the real cricket – wasn't up to much, and I only played two or three times when games were arranged as a result of goading by Sniffy. There were plenty of rubber planters around, some of whom had probably played some good cricket in their time; but a rubber planter is, or was, a very busy man. He would be out rousing his tappers at around 4.30 a.m. and getting them out onto their section areas, which he would patrol until about 9.30 a.m. when he'd return for breakfast. After that he'd be dealing with office and factory work until about 2 p.m. Later, if he was a good manager, he'd be down at the coolie lines on public relations visits. So even if a planter had been a cricketer, he would be woefully short of practice, and it has to be said that, despite Sniffy, Malacca cricket didn't really prosper.

Rugger was really the thing for the younger planters. They would travel 40 or 50 miles, often on their motorcycles, for a game, and then go on a 'thrash' until two or three in the morning, after which they would somehow weave their way home and be on parade on their estate at the proper time. I can only recall one unhappy result of this kind of jamboree: a planter, returning to his estate in the early hours went over the edge off the Singapore/Johore causeway and drowned in deep water. A friend of mine, Bill Galvin, dived in repeatedly in an effort to save him but couldn't find him.

Rugger was indeed almost, if not quite, as sancrosanct as cricket in Malaya. I recall one embarrassing occasion, however, which resulted from the not uncommon exuberance of the rugby player with a few drinks inside him. I had gone into Singapore for the weekend to play in an inter-state rugger match. Afterwards that evening we all went to the Victoria Theatre to see the play *Journey's End.* The actor playing the principal part had been taken ill and Noel Coward, who was visiting Singapore, agreed at very short notice to play the part. Not unnaturally he occasionally fluffed his lines, and some of the rugger 'hearties' in our midst were quite inexcusably rude to him. Coward was understandably furious, and I have heard it said that it was as a result of this disgraceful episode that he wrote *Mad Dogs and Englishmen'.*

I may say that I was a bit of a fraud as far as rugger went. I never really knew the game at all well. If somebody gave me the ball I used to run through sheer fright. But I was always ready in an emergency to make up the number.

Peddling my cigarettes, I came one day to a place in central Johore called Yong Peng. Today I see on the map that it is on the main road system, but at that time – 1929 – it was well off the beaten track. I walked up a steep hill to the village, where I went about my business. Then the shuttered window of a long wooden hut opened. A head popped out and a voice said, 'Come in and talk. We don't often see a white man here.' This turned out to be a medical missionary from Yorkshire, and he'd become a convinced British Israelite. He had the walls of his cabin decked out with maps and graphs and all kinds of statistics from the Flood down to the imminent Cataclysm that is apparently in store for many of us. His long-term graph showed what may well have been the rise of two world powers, one of which in due course dominated the other but eventually sank. The chart showed a curious reversal of proceedings. Could these, in retrospect, have been Russia and Germany?

I asked, 'What about France?'

'It sinks for a long time,' replied my host, 'but it emerges again at the top.'

'And Britain?' I asked.

'Britain has a leading world role to play because she is the Chosen Race. After the death of Solomon the Empire was divided; the northern half was Israel and it contained ten of the twelve tribes of the Israelites. These became "lost", but in fact the survivors settled in northern Europe, and we believe that the British are the Lost Ten Tribes, and in concert with America they are destined to rule the world and to bring it back into harmony with God . . .' I was rather glad to escape down the hill with my cigarettes. My last memory, as I backed away towards the car saying, 'Yes, yes,' was of my host standing there with his hand upraised in a kind of blessing, saying 'Believe.'

I remember telling the story to Sniffy, who said, 'I don't suppose the chap plays cricket.'

I must say that Gerald Scales wasn't a great deal of help to me in propagating the cricket 'Idea'. All he really wanted from me, as a brother Riff Raff, was to spend what he called a 'Raffish' evening. I didn't want this because he had a most delightful new young wife, Georgie, and when I went to the Scales ménage, all I wanted to do was to sit there and look at her, and I couldn't do this and be Raffish at the same time.

It was, however, at the Scales' house that I met one of the most remarkable men I've ever encountered. This was 'Lawyer' Cooper, who was certainly a first-class raconteur, even if some of his stories may have been exaggerated. According to his own version of events, he had enlisted before the turn of the century as a trooper in the ranks of a British cavalry regiment – a 'Gentleman Ranker' if ever there was one. Caught up in the Boer War, he had found himself in South Africa, and in due course was embroiled in the débacle at Spion Kop. Dismounted now, he had been an orderly runner to General Sir Charles Warren who, under the C-in-C, Sir Redvers Buller VC, was directing this disastrous operation. Cooper described the stream of orders and counter orders given by Warren and how on at least two occasions he climbed Spion Kop to give new instructions to the commander of the British forces caught at the top under withering Boer artillery and rifle fire.

There was, in this connection, Cooper's story about how he 'helped to lose the battle of Spion Kop' by getting himself Lost when carrying an important message from Warren to Buller. This episode might indeed be the one referred to in the official record: 'The orderly sent by Warren to Buller added one final touch to the tale of bungling by losing his way.' Warren had been seconded from the Army between 1886 and 1888 to be Commissioner of the Metropolitan Police. His reign had not been auspicious because, although he had been meticulous over administrative detail (he often sent out his orders in rhyming couplets), he seems to have been oblivious of the primary task of the police, which was then as now, to fight crime.

Among his many exploits Cooper claimed to have ridden with French (later Field Marshall Sir John French, and Earl of Ypres) in the epic ride with what remained of the cavalry division that hastened the surrender of the Boer General Cronje at Paardeberg. Cooper's stories went on and on, and memory fails over very many of them. He seems to have left the Army after the Boer War, only to rejoin – this time as an officer for service in World War One. After the war he read law, and by the time I met him he was established in a Singapore practice as a very able criminal lawyer.

Scales himself, conducting a one-sided Raffish evening, ended up almost under the table. I was to meet Cooper on several occasions later on during my travels, and I do recall his preoccupation with the teachings of the remarkable Rudolf Steiner, who wrote voluminously and lectured on a scientific approach to Life After Death. I think it must have been Cooper who first aroused my own very considerable interest, though this lay dormant for many years.

At about this time there was an embarrassing little incident. Scales had gone to Singapore for the weekend and had asked me to entertain his two ladies, Georgie and her sister. The incident occurred at the Malacca swimming pool, where all good Malaccans (Europeans) would have been present. A well-known and much revered member of the medical profession was disporting himself at the pool. He was wearing one of those old-fashioned bathing suits that has the disadvantage, for male wearers, of permitting the undercarriage to fall through, unless properly administered. The good doctor had not dealt with the problem at all satisfactorily, and there he was sitting on the edge of the pool waving happily to friends and acquaintances completely unaware that his bathing costume had let him down and that his 'unseeables' were in full view of the public. I was conscious of some discreet giggling between my two sisterly companions, and I didn't know which way to look. Eventually someone approached the doctor and pointed out the state of his dress. He immediately went to the bottom of the pool, emerging spluttering but decent.

The Malacca swimming club has one more memory for me. I had imported from a cruise ship a very beautiful but distinctly coffee-coloured young lady, and I took her to swim. I was aware that although envious male eyes were cast in my direction, there was some tut-tutting among some of the *Mem-Tuans.* Later I discussed the matter with Sniffy. He laughed and said, 'Good for you, but you know what a few of our ladies are like; we still have this infernal colour business.' Indeed we had. On one occasion at the Bukit Timur Golf Club, I asked a well-known local to play with me. We had our game, and I asked him to the clubhouse for a drink – a perfectly normal thing to do. But he wouldn't come, and I quickly realized that I'd been tactless. He had mixed blood, and I suppose he had probably had difficulties in the past and wasn't prepared to risk any further absurd rudeness. It was, I am afraid, all part of the social make-up of the colonies, and it was something I could never quite come to terms with.

I am reminded, too, of the Malacca golf course. Bukit Timur had been a delight, even for a very poor golfer such as I was. I had played a lot there, nevertheless, and was eventually able to get round fairly regularly in the late eighties. But Malacca put paid to all that; the fairways were very sandy, and such grass as there was existed in tufts and one had to hit the ball cleanly. I never got the trick; indeed my golf never recovered from Malacca. I used to play with a somewhat desolate and despondent solicitor called Cowper. One day a friend of mine – Gunter – was being given his first lesson in golf. Cowper and I were about 15 yards away on a putting 'brown'. Gunter, a large powerful man, let fly, and the ball hit poor Cowper bang in the midriff. 'Sorry,' said Gunter, 'I sliced.' In fact he had pulled the ball to square leg where we were putting, and there was Cowper, writhing on the ground.

Cowper was, in fact, a lonely man, and needed company. Accordingly, we would not infrequently have a Raffish evening after golf. On those occasions, not only did Cowper's eyes appear to vanish after several *Stengahs,* but he was the only man I ever met whose hair used literally to stand on end. Sometimes, after such an orgy, he would ring me in the morning and ask if I knew where he'd left his car. He'd been visiting friends overnight, he believed, and wasn't sure just where he'd been. All this, of course, was very many years before anyone thought about the undesirability of drinking and driving.

It was at this time that I made the acquaintance of N.H.P. Whitley, a puisne Judge and a mighty hitter of balls – cricket, golf and tennis. He had even captained England at lacrosse. I met him in the company of 'Lawyer' Cooper and had earlier seen him on the cricket field in Singapore. He smote Aeneas Perkins thrice in one over into the pavilion. He was the most modest of men. Years later he travelled out to East Africa on the same ship as my family and was very kind to my wife Elaine. He died in 1957, having spent the years from 1937 to 1947 as Chief Justice of Uganda.*

My Malacca days soon came to an end. Frank Hill and our Penang director visited us, and I was delighted to hear that I'd done a good job, but I was now to move on to Kuala Lumpur, from which – still selling cigarettes – I was to cover the three states of Selangor, Negri Sembilan and Pahang.

Reluctant as I was to leave Malacca, the move pleased me. I was getting to know something of the real Malaya. I took my leave of Sniffy, one of the great characters of my colonial years. Sadly I was never to meet him again, and I never heard much about how our cricket trainees were progressing – if indeed they did progress. As I was about to depart, my circle lost a genuine friend, you could say; our mascot: John Hinde's Scottie terrier, a game and devoted little creature, ran into the jungle within sight of its owner and was taken by a panther.

As I was to discover over very many years, final partings were the way of things in Colonial life; one just had to get used to them.

---

* Sir Norman Whitley. He won the MC at Gallipoli.

6

Tigers, Chuckers and 'Jonkers'

My new boss in Kuala Lumpur was Matthews. Not Mr Matthews or Sir. Just plain Matthews; I was plain Imray, of course.

His use of the English language centred on the word 'bloody'. It was almost his only adjective, and its constant use, I have to admit, rubbed off on me. To this day I use the word far more extensively and far less meaningfully than I should.

Almost his opening remark to me was, 'I want you to take over all the bloody presents, they're the bane of my bloody life. Come and have a look at them; they're taking up all the room in the bloody warehouse.'

What were these 'presents'? I hadn't encountered them in my cigarette dealings in Malacca. In fact, they were 'gimmicks' useless devices bought in quantity at the whim of some sales director or promotions manager to be given to customers and potential customers as, at best, goodwill gestures; at worst, as bribes.

There they were in serried ranks in the warehouse. A few of them were not too bad, but most were of no use to man or beast. It was all to do with the wretched cut-throat competition that always existed between the major manufacturers, especially between ourselves and the British American Tobacco Company, BAT, in which we, operating for Carreras, were always the losers.

At that time, Carreras had launched a new brand called

Piccadilly, in order to compete at a particular level with – if memory serves correctly – BAT's Ardath. If one ordered X amount of Piccadilly, one was liable to be presented with a toy pussycat on wheels. If Y amount was taken, you might get something mechanical that didn't work because the key had been lost or hadn't been supplied with the article. If you ordered half the stock in the warehouse, you might get a table lamp, with or without a bulb or plug.

I didn't like the look of it at all; it seemed far too much like hard, time-wasting work. However, I spent my first two weeks cataloguing the presents and putting sticky labels on them, which in Malaya's heat was a glutinous business.

The town (now city) of Kuala Lumpur lay in the centre of what was really a vast clearing in the middle of the Selangor jungle, though the jungle had been more and more infiltrated, as was the case throughout much of Malaya, by rubber plantations. The heat of these up-country regions away from the sea was cloying and damp. It sapped one's energy in a way I hadn't encountered before. There were no domestic refrigerators in those days, and air-conditioning hadn't then been thought of.

In KL much of the European social life revolved round the 'Spotted Dog'. This was the Selangor Club, which ran along one side of the sports ground, the *Padang*. On the other side, thoroughly picturesque in that eastern setting, were the Government offices. I was at once reminded of the Brighton Pavilion, which has always seemed to me incongruous in its western setting. However, there they were in KL, with their domes, colonnades and minarets adding scenic lustre to the place.

I'm not entirely sure why the Selangor Club was called the 'Spotted Dog', but the story was that in times gone by people of mixed blood had become members, and that the pejorative nickname was coined by colonials.

Most of the big companies had offices in Kuala Lumpur with its excellent sporting facilities, and there was a thriving Asian club which produced some fine cricketers.

Among them was Lall Singh, with whom I was to play much cricket. He was later, in 1932, to tour England with one of the first Indian representative teams. He was a fine fast-medium bowler and an attacking batsman of class. Lall was, indeed, the only cricketer in Selangor who dealt satisfactorily with the Chinese demon, Ping.

Ping had now transferred from Singapore to KL on some further education project or other, and it wasn't long before we were compelled to face him again on the cricket field. Seldom can such a small man have propelled a cricket ball off such a short run with such remarkable velocity and with such deadly accuracy, or with such an enchanting smile lighting up his face.

Ping's bowling action had been under close scrutiny by the Synod. He had been for a while under some suspicion of the diabolical sin of 'throwing'. However, he emerged from this dark cloud with colours flying, exonerated by the Synod and ready to strike fear into the hearts of batsmen far and wide.

We had, alas, no cricket personalities of the calibre of Sniffy and A.K., but we did have Guy Brand of the House of Harper Gilfillan. Brand was a fine wicketkeeper and forcing batsman who had played good cricket in England. He was the organizing genius of Selangor, but he had no Synod to help him, and there was no 'Riff Raff' on which to draw. Moreover, he was very much occupied with his business affairs. He inducted me into the ways of KL cricket, and for that I have always been grateful.

Another fine cricketer concealed somewhere in the depths of Selangor was 'Hoppy', Dr H.O. Hopkins, an Oxford Blue of the early 1920s who had turned out for Worcester. He appeared only rarely in our cricketing midst. I did play against him once, however, when he made a fine century, and there was no doubt about his class. Another splendid century at about this time came from R.N. Hamilton, a member of the Synod who was visiting from Singapore. R.N. had played minor county cricket in England and it was said that he had modelled his batting on

Jack Hobbs, whom he had known well. Certainly his display on the KL *Padang* was masterly and a joy to watch.

Ian Begley visited us *en route* to Penang, where he was now to be posted. We had a splendid evening together, spoiled only by a coarse fellow who called Begley 'Beggles, old boy' within minutes of meeting him. You just didn't do that kind of thing to the Begleys of the colonial world. It wasn't on.

I recall another little incident while Begley was with us. I introduced him to a Chinese friend of mine who prided himself on his knowledge of English quotations. I forget the subject under discussion, but turning to Begley he said: 'But my grandmother and I must try not to suck each other's eggs.' Begley's face was a study. 'Yes, Grandma would quite understand,' he said.

At Carreras we had a European resident 'rep' who made up the number on the cricket field when we were under strength, but for the life of me I can't remember his name. Anyway he was a delightful chap who was married to a most attractive Eurasian girl. For this reason he and his new wife were unable to mix in white society. I was fond of him and, of course, had met his wife and found her charming. What aggravated me most was the knowledge that the *Mem-Tuans*, the true power in the land, were probably to a large extent responsible for this outrageous social ostracism. I recall the matter because it was around this time that I read E.M. Forster's *A Passage to India*, and I still remember how it made me squirm.

An American acquaintance of my family was passing through KL while I was there, and I was appointed to show him round.

He was from Philadelphia, where in those days there was a thriving Philadelphian cricket club, and I recall seeing a report in the press of an English touring team playing against them. I was looking forward to entertaining him and perhaps to get him the odd game with one of our local sides. Unfortunately, 'Bloody' Matthews cut across my path.

Matthews was ill. 'Bloody fever again,' he said. 'You'll

have to do the bloody honours.'

It appeared that a 'rep' from one of the companies for whom we were agents, was due to arrive in KL, and I now had to meet and look after him too. My American friend had to look after himself more or less while I attended to the 'official' visitor, who had a somewhat alcoholic reputation. The reputation was well founded. He'd been 'Raffish' all the way out from England on the ship, and was in no state at all when he got to KL.

Indeed, after the first day he went to ground in his room at the Station Hotel, and I was put in charge of his welfare. It was clear that he was quite ill, and he was under the doctor for some time. He was able to rise from his bed to meet a particular train, however. I accompanied him to the station, and when the train came in there was the usual bustle, noise and shouting. The rep held up his hand and commanded 'Listen.' Then, after a moment or so, 'Thank God, the sentence has been commuted. The execution was due to take place tomorrow.' What he was listening to, I never discovered, but he obviously felt himself to be in dire trouble. The doctor eventually consigned him to hospital, and that was the last I heard of him.

It had not been long since Somerset Maugham travelled through the Far East and the Pacific, in search, it is often said, of material for his remarkable short stories. Some say that the characters were published with insufficient disguise and are clearly recognizable. Certainly, a few of the people and stories I came into contact with found close likenesses in some of that brilliant writer's yarns.

As the year 1930 drew into 1931, it was clear that the world was sinking ever deeper into a ferocious economic slump. Malaya was having a bad time.

It had been common knowledge for some while that our company was teetering on the brink of disaster. It had over-traded heavily in the halcyon years of the early 1920s, and had virtually been kept afloat, more in hope than expectation, by the Chartered Bank where there had been a huge overdraft, based on the company's excellent financial record in the past.

Now there came to us news that Frank Hill had pulled out and gone home. This was highly ominous. The price of rubber had plummeted almost to zero and a number of plantations, badly hit financially, were pulling in their horns and axeing their staff.

The number of jobless Europeans in the country was reaching an alarming figure. Many who had committed their lives to Malaya tried to hang on in the hope that things would improve. There was a limit to their capacity to sustain themselves without a regular pay packet, however, and there were stories of men being sent home DBS (Distressed British Subject). A middle-aged planter whom I had met up-country, never made the voyage to England. He pitched himself over the rail in the Indian Ocean. Stories of American stockbrokers flinging themselves from sky-scraper windows on the realization that they had lost everything in the stock market depression had their sad parallels all over the western world; not least in Singapore and Malaya.

A tragi-comic case concerned a planter who tried to hang himself by jumping off the top balcony of the Sungei Ujong Club in Seremban, having tied a pyjama cord around his neck. The cord broke, and he ended up with a broken leg and a stiff neck.

At Port Dixon on the east coast a camp was set up for distressed Europeans. This, however, could only be a temporary palliative, and I believe it had to be closed down after only a few months. The Sword of Damocles continued to hang threateningly over my own company. Despite warning signs and all these tribulations, however, my time had not yet come, and I continued my very pleasant life of travelling around my vast territory, playing cricket and other games in season, meeting new people and enjoying myself enormously.

There was a company car, a Chevrolet, always at my disposal, and there was the long thin mournful-looking

Ahmed, the Malay *syce,* who was in fact a most resourceful person.

On one of our journeys, travelling for miles across Pahang, we had two tyre blow-outs. Nothing daunted, on the second occasion, when we were without a spare, Ahmed stuffed the outer cover with grass, sealed the whole thing with latex from a rubber tree and enabled us to limp in to Kuala Lumpur where, because we had to send for extra tyres, we had to spend two of the hottest and most airless nights I can ever recall down by the river.

While Ahmed attended to our first puncture and changing the wheel (the car was his business and he would not allow interference in its welfare), I had walked down the road and into a jungle clearing, where I sat down on a log and watched a glorious cloud of butterflies. And then, to my astonishment, there was a grunt and rustle in the tall grass and out came a wonderful tiger, not 15 yards away from me. It didn't seem to see me, and I kept dead still and watched it stalk down to a little stream, have a drink and a scratch and go on its way.

Curiously, I wasn't frightened, just enormously uplifted by the splendid sight. The Malayan tiger is a tawny colour and smaller, I believe than the Bengal species, but still very much a tiger.

There was never a problem over accommodation for travellers. The Rest Houses in these regions bore no comparison with those I was to know much later on in Africa. In Malacca, for example, the so-called Rest House was the equivalent of a small hotel, and in Johore there were two very presentable places, while even in Pahang at a place called Raub, there was a quite excellent establishment where, as at most other places, everything was provided and you could always get a meal.

There was a very pleasant stop-off point on my Selangor circuit. This was at Frazer's Hill, some 2,500 feet above the steaming jungle surrounds. It was at that time the only hill station in Malaya, and people used to stay there at a branch of the Selangor Club. Fires were lit, and men and women tended to walk around dressed in plus fours and tweed skirts, pretending they were in Europe. The temperature was much more pleasant than down below, but one was still very much in the tropics, whatever devices the colonials might use to pretend otherwise.

On one of my visits to Frazer's Hill, the topic of conversation at the club was of a tigress and two cubs in full possession of one of the golf club tees. My informant had not interrupted the family party.

I played plenty of cricket in KL. However there was no Sniffy Clark to get things done., Cricket needs men like Sniffy if it is to thrive in the backblocks, and I hope that if cricket is still played in Singapore and Malaysia, someone has thought to erect a statue to Sniffy, and indeed to A.K.

Such grandiose thoughts aside, there were sometimes games of good class and, as usual in the Colonies, there was a good deal of cricket 'ideology'.

There was a small cricket school in KL. I was on friendly terms with two young police officer cadets, and we played together occasionally on the *Padang.* I was often invited to their Mess. One of the cadets, Freddie Caldwell, used to run a net where he instructed the police rank and file in the cricket arts and crafts, and sometimes I was pulled in to help. But that was really my only contribution towards spreading the gospel during the KL period.

There was a memorable brush with an ideologue up in Ipoh (pronounced Eepo), where I was playing for Selangor against Perak (pronounced Peera). I hadn't done very well with the bat; I was out trying a lofted off-drive and was caught – as happened to me time and again – at deep mid-off. However I took several wickets with my off-spinners and was lectured at some length on my cricket by a long, lean, craggy South African by the name of Jonklaas. Inevitably he came to be known in those remote cricketing circles as 'Jonkers', a man much respected for his knowledge of the game and for his almost religious devotion to it.

I was to meet Jonkers later in KL. He did a bit of newspaper journalism in his spare time, and I recall that he took me to task in the local paper in a kindly, though casutic, fashion. He thought, for example, that I should learn to bowl my off-spinners on the off-side of the wicket. I had been practising the 'wrong-un', with the result that I lost direction, put the ball somewhere about middle stump and very short of a length, and was hoiked away for a succession of sixes. It was perceptive of Jonkers, and as soon as I could get to the police cadets' nets I practised until I could turn the delivery from about middle and off, and from then on claimed a number of wickets.

One day, playing on the *Padang* at KL, I met Andrew Mustard. He planted rubber on an estate called Bukit Jalil, about seven to ten miles outside KL, off what was then the Klang/Port Swettenham road. The estate was well into the jungle.

Here was another of cricket's 'characters'. He had just returned from a lengthy furlough in Britain, and had had to leave his wife behind when he returned. I was just vacating an unsatisfactory lodging, and Andrew asked me to join him on his estate from which, when in KL, I could commute daily to and from the office.

The 45-year-old, ever-laughing Andrew was a born practical joker, sometimes to the point of being a nuisance, and stories about him abounded. He had evidently turned out in the past for Somerset, and there at Bukit Jalil, cricket was very much on his mind. The Tamil foreman of his workforce was called Iddumun, and he had been recruited by Andrew into joining the cricket fraternity. Andrew said he needed to keep in practice, so he had rigged up a net and Iddumun was coerced into bowling.

As it transpired, the Tamil turned out to be a natural 'chucker'. Every ball was a near unplayable throw, and a very accurate one at that. Andrew would place a few cents on the stumps, and every time Iddumun hit them the money would be his, which he thought an excellent idea. He hadn't a pocket, so he put his winnings in his mouth. Of course I was expected to add my mite both to the fun and to Iddumun's fast increasing wealth. Before long we had quite an audience from Andrew's workforce, and we even enlisted a couple of recruits who, by the time I left the scene, were making very fair progress, though they were unable to deliver anything like Iddumun's lethal ball, and so were unable to enrich themselves.

Thus did Andrew foster cricket in the jungle. I remember him joking, 'Don't tell anyone about Iddumun's throwing or I'll be drummed out of the MCC.'

Whatever Lords might have thought of it, Andrew's planter neighbours were soon facing the redoubtable Iddumun. After all, a bowler was a bowler in the jungle, and umpires weren't at all fussy about the more esoteric laws of the game. I don't ever recall him being no-balled.

There came the moment of a long-planned five-a-side, single-wicket competition, got up between Andrew's and Bereford's select representatives. The event was to celebrate Andrew's 45th birthday.

For Andrew himself there was Iddumun, the two police cadets, Freddie and Coxy, and me.

Beresford, who had played for Harrow at Lords, had imported 'Hoppy', an Indian, another planter, a Wykehamist (none of whose names I remember), and to the horror of our men - the redoubtable Ping, brought over from his Kuala Lumpur establishment.

The match was played on Andrew's tennis court, heavily netted on the jungle side. The outfield sloped away steeply so that the 'wicket' was at the top of the hill, as it were, and the bowler appeared suddenly over the brow and was only visible at the moment of delivery. All players on both sides fielded, apart from the batsman, of course, but most of them were out of sight of the actual proceedings in the middle. The umpire was Frank Mustard, Andrew's brother.

The mayhem that both Iddumun and Ping might wreak under these conditions was not hard for the players on either side to imagine. Both teams employed two long stops - very necessary, because the wicketkeeper, in order to be in touch with play, had to stand close to the stumps. Frank Mustard blew a whistle as each ball was delivered so that fielders were given advance warning.

Beresford won the toss and batted. Iddumun was lethal. The Indian was laid low, Hoppy and Beresford himself were clean bowled, or at any rate 'thrown', and only Ping and the Wykehamist managed a few snicks. There were 16 byes in a total of 24. We did even worse, making 17, Ping doing the damage. The second innings performances were much the same as the first, and when proceedings came to an end there were so many wounded figures that the two captains decided a draw was the only fair result. We all repaired to Andrew's house for ample refreshment, except for Iddumun, who had skulked away, deciding, it was later reported, that there was no point in playing cricket if there was no coinage on the stumps. Andrew was said to have paid him a 'benefit' bonus.

I played quite a few games for Andrew's XI. All things considered, his fixtures produced some very good cricket against composite teams raised from various districts and organizations. There were my two police cadet friends, both excellent cricketers, and Andrew's brother Frank, who although in his mid-fifties, was still a very useful performer. He, too, had played for Somerset. Andrew even enlisted Ping for a couple of matches, and there was a very useful Indian spinner in the side. I think we won each of the games, even against a good Services team from Singapore, and there was a strong side from Penang, which very nearly beat us as a result of some wily bowling by none other than my friend Begley, now based in Penang.

There came a somewhat alarming episode. Several Tamil tappers had been killed on Bukit Jalil and on neighbouring estates. It was clear that a man-eating tiger was at large, and something had to be done about it.

The planters got together. A rentice was cut in the jungle and some careful reconnaissance work was done – rather on the lines of Exmoor stag-hunting, when the harbourer goes out very early to locate a'warrantable' stag. Thus some idea of the tiger's 'beat' was gleaned. It was believed to lie up in some rocky ground on an estate that was adjacent to us at Bukit Jalil.

A day was arranged and the planters assembled. The plot was for planters armed with rifles to stand along the rentice, a narrow cleared path in the jungle, at 50-yard intervals. Parties of 'beaters' with a pack of dogs were posted in the jungle some half-mile or so behind the rocky outcrop. They were to beat tin cans and make as much noise as possible, hoping to get the tiger moving towards the rentice, where the planters stood waiting. I was posted at the far end of the picket line, and all I had was a double-barrelled shotgun with a metal ball stuck up one spout and some buckshot in the other; ludicrously inadequate if I were to be confronted by the tiger.

Although it was considered that in my position I would probably be out of harm's way, I complained to Andrew, who was alongside me.

'It's all right,' he said, 'I'll be covering you, and in any case if the tiger appears all you need to do is to let it get really close and then blaze off.'

I didn't like it at all.

Everything was made ready, and the 'fun' started. The beaters were making one hell of a noise with their tin cans. Andrew by this time was 50 yards away, yakking to one of the planters at the next picket post. What was I to do, I wondered, if the tiger surfaced near me?

I duly moved into position. Then I froze in horror. The *lallang* in front of me was moving, and something was coming through it.

I prayed, 'Oh, please God, don't let it be the tiger.' Then out onto the rentice came a large shaggy dog, one of the planters' canines. It saw me and wagged its tail.

There came an unmistakable noise from way out in the jungle ahead of us, followed by the yelping and crying of a dog. Then there was a shot.

What had happened was that the tiger had broken back through the line of beaters, clawing a dog badly as it did so. A planter had then shot the unfortunate dog, which was dying anyway, and the tiger escaped in the mélee. However, our operation must have been successful, because during my time at least, there were no more attacks on rubber planters.

On a happier note, it was on Bukit Jalil that I first encountered that extraordinary and, even then, rare animal, the tapir.

About the size of a small donkey, grey to black in colour, it has a kind of shortened elephant trunk. I woud have thought that these creatures would be easy meat for tigers and panthers, but Andrew assured me, 'They pong. No self-respecting tiger would touch them unless it was very hungry.'

It might be thought that we were an almost entirely male society, but that was far from being the case. The opposite sex was well represented. One very glamorous woman, probably in her thirties, frequented the 'Spotted Dog' for a while. She spoke a somewhat 'Continental' brand of English, didn't appear to have any attachments, and nobody seemed to know what she was doing in KL. Andrew said firmly that she was a spy and that I should bring her up to Bukit Jalil and make her bat against Iddumun. He was probably thinking hopefully of a new-found version of the beautiful Mata Hari.

I thought it improbable that anybody would find it worthwhile to do any spying in KL, but Andrew's improbable observations often proved to contain more than a grain of truth.

I used to dance at the 'Dog' sometimes with an attractive young brunette, Suzie, and even took her out to Andrew's place for lunch. She was staying a while with a highly respectable uncle and aunt in KL. About a year later in London, together with a Malayan friend of mine, Bill Galvin, I was in a fashionable *Palais de Dance*, and there, doing a hostess job, was Suzie. I tried to fix a date, but her eyes were roving and Bill whispered, 'Don't you realize she's on the game?'

What an innocent I was.

The other woman whom I recall distinctly was the enormous blonde wife of a jockey. She used to get most deplorably drunk at the 'Dog'. She was usually on her own and tacked onto any party she could find. The business of getting her home was difficult, and there needed to be two for the job, not only to assist her into a car but also to face the ire of the jockey if he was at home and not away jockeying.

I suppose we all do silly things at times. But even now, after some 60 years, I wonder to myself, 'Can I really have been so stupid?'

I had been called down to Singapore on business matters, and I spent a long weekend there. Joining up with some Riff Raffs, we found ourselves eventually at a dowmmarket place of entertainment called 'The Wide World'. Amongst other attractions there was a boxing booth, and standing in the ring was a Philippino called Kim the Killer. It was announced that anybody who could last three two-minute rounds against the Killer would receive 100 Straits dollars. Now I hardly knew a thing about boxing, but I had read about Regency pugilism, and there was a character called 'The Croucher' who had captured my imagination.

The Croucher's techique was to fold himself in half and, hiding his head with his arms, whilst presenting only his left side towards his opponent, he would then bore in. At the opportune moment he would deliver a devastating punch to the ribs. Incredible to relate, and to the horror of my fellow Riff Raffs, I stood up and challenged the Killer. I was rigged up in some smelly kit provided by the management, and we started.

The first round wasn't too bad. Everybody, including the Killer, laughed at my Croucher antics. The Killer had obviously decided I was easy meat and that he could pick me off at will, and the audience had to be entertained.

However, in round two, boring in with the kind of zeal that might have pleased the Croucher, I made the mistake of having a crack at the Killer's ribs. I got him a bit low, and this riled him. I should have been disqualified, but I was to be the burnt offering and, come what may, I was going to be laid out cold. Anyway, the Killer had had enough of my prancing around, and he was going to finish the job. The third round was devastating, and my arms, protecting my head, were being punched to a pulp. But incredibly I managed to hold out, and the 100 dollars were mine.

I was the hero of the hour, and the money only just outlasted the rest of the evening as the Riff Raffs celebrated. It took several days for my arms to recover from the pounding.

I was accompanied on a visit to Kuantan on the east coast of Pahang by one Bulloch, a mighty rugger man who had had a trial for Scotland. Even in that Malaya heat he always wore a London Scottish tie.

At Beserah, on the sea shore a couple of miles or so from Kuantan, we stopped at the Rest House and there encountered a highly civilized French aristocrat who introduced himself as the Vicomte du Bondé. He asked us to join him and his Malay lady friend for dinner, and he personally cooked a most splendid curry. He regretted the absence of whisky but made up for it with an excellent wine, toasting his lady charmingly in French before departing into the night on a sea fishing excursion, leaving us and his lady on the beach.

7

Kuala Rompin

In KL one day Matthews said to me, 'You know those bloody Green Lady cigarettes in the warehouse?'

'Can't say I do,' I replied.

'They've been there for about a year, and we haven't sold a bloody tin. They're horrible bloody cigarettes, of course, and I've just had a call from Singapore telling me to get rid of them.'

'Ah, ha ha,' I said weakly, wondering what scheme might be runing through Matthews's mind.

'You're the bloody cigarette man, and I'm leaving the details to you, but what I would suggest is that you get over to the east coast and try and sell the bloody things in some of those villages down through Pahang to Johore . . .'

Here was another glorious opportunity to get away from it all and to see more of Malaya – the real Malaya. Stacking the Green Lady, cases and cases of the things onto a lorry and myself travelling as usual in the company car, I took the normal route through Pahang, ended up at Kuantan, and thence south to Pekan.

There I chartered a fairly derelict old barge, loaded the Green Lady and put out to sea. I had a fair idea of the location of villages down the coast, and I had with me our Kuantan agent, a great fat Chinese *towkay* who would get a good rake-off from Green Lady sales. Hugging the coast and stopping off here and there whenever it was possible, over the next two or three days we were doing a fair trade. The

Green Lady, sold at a discount, were dirt cheap, and the villagers actually seemed to like the wretched things. Then, very close inland, and approaching Kuala Rompin, we ran into trouble and the *serang* (master of the boat) said he didn't like the look of the weather.

Neither did I. The rain was coming down in sheets, and the sea was heaving us about. The remaining cases of Green Lady – and there were still a number left – were all under the hatch, but there wasn't much cover for us. We carried on for a bit until, through the rain, we saw Kuala Rompin village, and almost at the same time we hit a sandbank. The boat started to clap up and down, and it looked as though she might break in half. There was nothing for it but to abandon ship and swim for the shore; we were only about 200 yards or so from safety. The *towkay* said he couldn't swim. I got him to the edge, gave him a shove, and over he went, splosh. I went in after him, and he bobbed up like a cork. I took hold of him round his fat belly – it was rather like trying to hold on to the underside of a porpoise – and we paddled to the beach, with the *towkay* spluttering all the way.

When finally we reached the beach, gasping for breath, I asked, 'What was that you were trying to say?'

'Ikan yo' (shark), he replied.

He explained later that, although he hadn't actually seen one, he was afraid there might be one.

The *serang* and his mate were not far behind us, and they too made for the beach safely. The villagers were kind and gave us food and shelter, and we dried ourselves.

So there we were, wearing borrowed plumes (*sarong* and *baju*) and hopelessly cut off from all known sources of succour. Behind the village lay miles and miles of jungle, and of course there were no telephones or telegraph – indeed, no means of communication whatever.

I sat down and considered our position. I had to admit that the prospect looked unhealthy. I had wanted very much to see the real Malaya, and now it seemed that I was in its grip.

The *penghulu* (headman) wasn't very cheering. There was,

of course, the river, he told us. This went up through 'the city' (the main Rompin village) and then on into the jungle, to Allah alone knew where. Two of his people had taken the river some months ago, but there had been no news of them since.

In the meantime he gave me a basin of leaves. 'Rub the juice into your skin,' he said, 'the *serangga* (insects) won't worry you.' I found this most effective, and I've always cursed that I didn't make a note of the native name for the substance. I was given to understand that the aboriginal Sakhai always used this treatment.

From what the *penghulu* told us, it seemed that we must have struck the back end of a 'Sumatra' – one of those sudden, very violent storms that are prevalent in South-East Asia.

Next day the weather had cleared, and although our future seemed as uncertain as ever, I felt more buoyant in spirit, though I had to admit a whisky would have made me feel better still. Then the *penghulu* reappeared with somebody called Tukang Beri Ubat, who I discovered was the 'Dispenser'. He explained that should we need drugs or treatment there was in fact a dispensary in KR, and that once a month a 'doctor' came from somewhere to look after the sick, but as he'd only just been and gone, he wouldn't be back for a while.

I looked around me; the tide was low, and there – astonishingly – was our craft high and dry on the sandbank. The *serang* went out in a canoe to investigate and his report was gloomy. There was damage and he would have to try and repair it, but this might take some while, and even then he wasn't sure whether we could make it back to Pekan.

I took a sudden firm decision. Come what may, the Green Lady cigarettes – if indeed they had survived – were not going to travel any further; they'd given us enough trouble already. Circumstances were clearly such that we couldn't fuss about the commercial aspect; we would give the damned things away.

I explained our position to the *penghulu* and told him that the Green Lady were his to dispense among his people. I hoped that they had not been too damaged by their ordeal, and now would he kindly arrange a fatigue party and have them brought in from the boat to the shore.

Of course he was delighted to accept the offer, and a fatigue party went out to the stranded boat. Then I suddenly remembered our cigarette takings; they were in a bag stuffed behind the cases of Green Lady under the poop, lying on a sort of ledge. It was quite a considerable sum. What if the fatigue party lifted it? Anyway, did it really matter, considering the mess we were in?

Nonetheless, I hired a canoe and paddled out ostensibly to see how our *serang* was getting on with the repairs, and there, mercifully, was my bag of money.

Ashore, it soon became clear that our Green Lady cigarettes were popular. Almost everyone in the village, young and old, male and female, was smoking them – sometimes two at a time.

In the meantime I had got to wondering how on earth I was going to fill in the time before we could either be rescued or take to sea again in the hope of reaching Pekan.

Then it came to me – cricket. I would teach the locals to play.

How pleased Aubrey Wallich, Sniffy and A.K. would be if they only knew of my enterprise!

But how to assemble the necessary equipment? Clearly, we would have to improvise. I went into lengthy conference with the *penghulu.* I called him *Guru Besar Sekolah* (Headmaster), which I think pleased him. Anyway, he had first to learn something of cricket himself and then help me to pass it on to his people.

We hatched a scheme. He sent somebody up a tree to find some suitable coconuts that would have to do duty as cricket balls if deftly operated on with a hatchet. We could perhaps use a tree of the same approximate width as a set of stumps, or maybe somebody could find three straight sticks from somewhere. There was no problem about this.

The bat presented some difficulty, however, and the

penghulu scratched his head; then he persuaded his Prime Minister – or Second Master – to get busy on a palm frond. It was cut down to the wood, and finally there emerged an implement that wasn't too far removed from the kind of bat one sees in photographs with a bearded gentleman in a top hat leaning on it. Admittedly it looked more like a hockey stick than a cricket bat, but we would have to adapt our game to the raw material available. This was going to be cricket in the backblocks as it should be played.

I paced out 22 yards over a fairly flat surface, and then we got a fatigue party to stamp it down hard. After that it was simply a matter of the *Guru* and I giving a demonstration, and of course we had the entire village watching, most of them still puffing at 'Glin Leddy' cigarettes.

'Bat' in hand, I took guard in front of the tree, and the *Guru* bowled the coconut along the ground, trying to hit the tree. I scored about half a dozen runs by hockey-sticking the coconut away on the leg side. Then I got bowled by one that came off a thick hairy seam. By this time everybody wanted to have a go with both bat and ball, and we had two ladies keeping wicket and stopping the ball with their *sarongs.*

I remember having a bit of trouble explaining the LBW rule, and inevitably we had a large number of run-outs – enough, I should have thought, to merit inclusion in the *Guinness Book of Records.*

Every one got hooked on 'clickit'. But all good things have to come to an end. The *serang* announced somewhat mournfully that he had done what he could and was prepared to essay the journey back to Pekan. In fact, he must have done a remarkable job.

As always in the backblocks, I never cease to be astonished at the ingenuity and improvisation of the local people in all kinds of difficult situations.

In any event, supplies of Green Lady were beginning to run out, and I sensed that the locals were beginning to get bored with having to give us board, lodging and clothing. So once again waiting for the middle tide, and with most of the village pushing, we were at last propelled amid frenzied cheers into deep water. The ancient engine purred, and away we went.

When we swam ashore at Kuala Rompin I was wearing a long Malvern scarf around my neck. It had dried nicely in the sun, and on our departure I presented it to the *Guru* as a thank-you offering for his hospitality. He wound it round his head and tied it firmly in a knot at the back. He had a good sense of humour and said, 'Now I really am a *Guru Besar Sekolah*.'

Lying down on the bottom boards, I went to sleep and didn't wake up until many hours later. It was dark, and we were approaching Pekan. Reviewing our adventures, I thought of the several occasions at Kuala Rompin when a coconut fell off a tree and hit the ground with a loud 'plop'. I have often wondered about this when I have been in coconut areas. The local people, I need hardly add, don't wear tin hats, and yet fatal accidents seem to be a rarity.

My return to KL didn't seem to produce the interest that I was expecting. After all, here I was virtually back from the dead. Matthews simply said: 'So here you are, back at bloody last. You don't need to tell me about the bloody Green Lady; it doesn't much matter now. The bloody company has folded up at last; Syme Darby have taken us over, and you and I have got the bloody sack.'

I was to remain in Malaya for another six or seven weeks, handing over my job to somebody in Syme Darby, with whom, for the last time, I toured the territory doing instroductions to the *towkays,* and saying goodbyes.

I had always been on friendly terms with our competitors. Both they and we knew that my company was on a losing wicket, that inevitably they would be the outright winners.

Guy Brand sent me a message to say there might be a job for me with his firm, Harper Gilfillan, but I decided to accept my present company's offer of a passage back to the United Kingdom. I would take two months' leave and would then pay my own way back to Malaysia, where with luck the job would be still waiting for me. And so I took my leave of that lovely part of the world where I had so thoroughly enjoyed myself.

8

In the Doldrums

It was November 1931. My family lived at Norbury, only about 15 minutes by train from Victoria Station. They welcomed me, and I was secure in the knowledge that there was plenty of room in the family home. They were my anchorage, but I went into London on most days, searching vainly to find a suitable job.

Homecoming was not exactly a new experience. Like most of the sons of even modestly well-off middle-class families, I had been away at prep and public schools for as long as I could remember, and going home between terms was always something of an anticlimax.

Indeed, my relationship with my parents, though it never lacked respect or admiration on my part, was never warm. Perhaps I should say a word or two here about them and their backgrounds.

My family, the Imrays, originated somewhere near Inverness, and a sub-clan fought for the Scottish Prince at Culloden. One of them escaped Cumberland's dragoons and reached London, where he set up a cartographic business. The firm flourished for nearly two centuries until in 1914, the Admiralty took over all substantial chart and map-making work. Hard times followed, and the family's fortunes diminished. But they had done well over the years, and even in my youth the firm still traded in a small way in London's Minories. There were eight children in my father

Herbert's generation, two boys and six girls; my father and his brother apparently loathed each other.

By the time I came along, most of my father's share in the family fortune had disappeared. As a young man in prosperous times he had completed at least two Grand Tours, taking in North Africa as well as the European capitals. He had also seen the Empire, in the shape of Australia and New Zealand. My earliest memories of him go back to about 1912. Tall, clean-shaven and slightly ginger-haired, dressed in frock coat and seldom far removed from the whisky bottle, he would pace his study at our Surrey home, where open books, diagrams, maps and charts betrayed his wide interest in the world and his abundant theories about history and government. At the age of three I would be called in to listen to his erudite commentaries – he had been introduced to the ageing Emperor Franz Josef and had met Cecil Rhodes – whom he revered – and so my early lessons were interlaced with fascinating stories of the good and the great of a fast-disappearing world.

The diminishing family fortunes and the frustrations that came with it undoubtedly encouraged his attachment to the bottle, and he died in the mid-sixties, but he had been a fair cricketer, tennis player and golfer in his day, and his knowledge of world affairs was considerable.

There was money too on my mother Mercie's side, the Allens. It came largely from property. My mother had been schooled at Roedean and 'finished' in Germany. Her father had strongly disapproved of mine as an in-law. My mother had a hard time with my father, poor woman. Accustomed to a life of some ease and privilege in her younger day, she was overshadowed by my father and had to bring up three children on very little money – much of what there was went on drink – and my abiding memory of her is of her seeming to be terribly tired and burnt out. She lived to 91, however, and thankfully her circumstances improved greatly after my father's death.

The reader may understand from this brief family note why travel and the wide-open spaces of the world appealed to me, and why for me home was never more than a temporary refuge.

Anyway, here I was back in England, lodging with the family in the suburbs and missing badly the 'colour' of Malaya. A cable had arrived from KL to the effect that, after all, I could not be employed at Harper Gilfillan.

Between Norbury and London I saw endless rows of drab houses, from which, no doubt, the 'nine to five' workers had been coming and going for years on end, without much prospect of change in their lives. Perhaps very many of them had reached a degree of contentment, but the safe and predictable life was not for me.

I visited my late company's London office, where I had worked for a few months before leaving for Malaya. At that time I had copied orders, checked invoices – usually getting the figures wrong because I was thinking of something else – and doing the kind of jobs that everyone else disdained.

Now, four years later, most of the staff were still there. Their jobs had not been affected by the closure of my company, because they were forwarding agents for several establishments in the Straits and were also affiliated to the big tin merchants who lived upstairs.

The liftman said, 'Haven't seen you lately. Been on your holidays, I suppose.'

I wanted to get some news of Dorothy, who, it will be remembered, had taken a job in the London office. I found I had only missed her by a couple of weeks or so.

I enquired of her from Miss Hawksley, who had been there crashing away at a typewriter since time began. She pursed her lips, and I felt at once that there was something I had to know.

In the hope of plumbing the depths of office scandal, I took Martin, the office 'boy', out for a drink. He was, in fact, a man of 26 or so years, but was still dogsbody to everyone because he was too good-hearted. He told me the story. The saga of Dorothy had, it seemed, become an office talking point that had superseded all others.

'I could see,' said Martin, 'that old Simmons (he was the financial man) had his eye on her; used to take her out to lunch sometimes, and they'd meet after office hours.'

Martin took a long draft of mild and bitter, pursed his lips and visibly gathered together the strands of his tale.

'Then Mrs S. came in one day all the way from Esher to see what was what, and she caught them together in a tea shop. Somebody must have peached; wouldn't be surprised if it wasn't Ma Hawksley. Old Simmons hasn't been the same since.'

Martin expanded. 'Poor Simmons; he'd been badly knocked about at Ypres and his wife was reputed to be a dragon.'

There was more. 'What about "Boy" Brown?' I asked. Brown was Martin's sidekick.

'He took a liking to Dorothy,' said Martin, 'and when he saw old Simmons cashing in he couldn't stand it no more and went and joined the Air Force. Even the reps used to come in specially to look at her when there weren't no business. Lucky we had old Prosser here; he calmed things down a bit.'

Prosser was the shipping man and the much-respected mainspring of the office. There was no doubt that the glamorous Dorothy had made an impact. I remembered how she used to talk to me about her 'natural suntan'. I could just imagine the impact she made in London.

Martin promised me he would ferret out anything he could find about Mr Maconochie, whom I remembered with affection. There was nothing to show how or why he had left Singapore so suddenly, but I was given a last-known address in Dundee. I managed to phone him, and there he was with his usual happy laugh.

He had not, he told me, been married to his Singapore 'wife'. Anyhow, she had vanished and he was now properly married to the lady to whom he had for years been paying a monthly stipend for breach of promise. 'She's rich,' said Mr Maconochie, 'and she's returned all the money she took off me.' He said he spent most of his time nowadays fishing, and why didn't I come and join him. I very nearly did, but not quite. I've never been a fisherman or wanted to fish. I told him about Dorothy, and he said enigmatically that he wasn't surprised.

There was no word about his exit from Singapore. We parted on very amiable terms.

In those days the Trocadero restaurant was 'upmarket' and beyond my slender means. However, it had a Long Bar where people from overseas used to gather. There was a book in which, if you wanted to meet your friends, you wrote your name, address and telephone number.

Thus it was that I contacted my friend Bill Galvin and several other Malayans, all of whom were jobless in Britain.

We each had a little – a very little in my case – 'retirement' money, but much of this was evaporating and the future looked bleak. It was at about this time, also that I ran into Norman Whitley at the 'Troc'.

Thereafter we met on several occasions, and he gave me lunch at his Club. At his suggestion I explored two possibilities. It seemed that recruitments were sometimes made for the Burmese teak forests. The salary offered looked princely, but the wastage rate for employees was high on account of the unhealthy areas where one was required to work.

I was full of malaria – I wasn't to lose it for some years – and the interviewing panel wanted me to go into the hospital for tropical diseases and get fixed up. I fought shy of treatment and of Burma, However. I've since wondered whether I should have been sensible, rid myself of the curse of malaria and gone to the Burma forests. My thoughts on the subject were reinforced a few years ago when I met a man well into his nineties who had been through the entire Burma gamut, survived everything climate and the Japanese could throw at him, and was as rich as Croesus. For his years he was as fit and active as could be.

Not to be put off by my indecisiveness, Whitley gave me a

note of introduction to an Assistant Commissioner at Scotland Yard, a distinguished ex-army officer. I could come into his office as a clerk, he said, though the pay would be derisory, and as soon as an opportunity occurred, he might be able to get me enlisted at Peel House as a recruit in the Metropolitan Police. He told me, however, that promotion in the force was slow and very competitive, as there were some very good men in the ranks.

I went away and digested this. I looked at grey, drizzling London, and it seemed to me, even in my jobless state, that anything would be preferable to pounding a beat round London's dismal streets with only an off-chance of ever getting away into higher realms of law enforcement.

Nonetheless, this interview and the Scotland Yard atmosphere did do something for me; I really believe it sparked off within me an interest in the police service, because forthwith I went to a library and started reading all about it.

It was late autumn, and the cricket season was still a long way ahead. In anticipation of being in England for some time, I joined a cricket school that belonged to Strudwick of Surrey. This was not my first experience of schools, as in 1927 I applied for membership of the Hampstead Nomads' Club and was well received. And it was at their suggestion that I went on that previous stay in England, to a famous indeed outstanding, indoor cricket school at Walham Green, run by the great South African G.A. Faulkner, who had played in the famous 1912 'Triangular Test' series between England, Australia and South Africa.

I went week after week to the Faulkner nets, and through the Nomads and the school I came into contact with some well-known cricketers, including A.P.F. Chapman, a very large young man who had only very recently captained England against Australia in the vital winning match at the Oval and two County captains - C.J.T. Pool of Northants and J.C. Clay of Glamorgan. Then there was Ian Peebles, later to play on occasions for England. I may be wrong, but I have an idea that G.T.S. Stevens of Middlesex and England was with us on several occasions. It is recorded that Stevens had been the only schoolboy cricketer of modern times to play for the Gentlemen against the Players. There was, too, a very good cricketer whom I got to know called F.J. Weeks, who had played on occasion for Gloucestershire.

Among the celebrities associated with Faulkner as co-directors of the school were such cricketing celebrities as H.D.G. Leveson-Cower and 'Plum' Warner, though they were very much in the background.

There were four nets at Walham Green, and there were of course some distinctions between 'Uppers' and 'Lowers', which included me; but we did get some of the top-class people bowling at us. I think it must have been at this time that Peebles was employed by Faulkner at the school, as he was usually there in a coaching capacity, and he was particularly helpful to the likes of me.

I recall another fine South African cricketer who came and went. That was S.J. Pegler, from Faulker's own territory, the Transvaal. I had the impression they were business associates. I had seen Pegler at the Oval in 1924 when, throughout that South African tour, he had been one of his country's key bowlers. He played a total of 16 Tests for South Africa. He took a hand at the nets with us once when I was there and, as with Faulkner, his bowling was an education.

They said of Faulkner at the school that he never bowled 'down' to his pupils, whether they were class cricketers or mere enthusiasts like me. He had matting wickets stretched over a wooden base, and would put a ball down time after time in almost exactly the same spot, but I found him impossible to read - despite his exhortations to watch his hand. Sometimes the ball would spin away, and then in would come the next one viciously. I suppose, looking back, I was being given the finest batting practice that a young man could hope for. Sadly, I did not capitalize on it as I might have done.

Who, then, was this Aubrey Faulkner?

I recall, after nearly 70 years, a large bulky man with a black moustache. He would then, according to *Wisden,* have been about 43 years old. I seem to remember that he had a fairly tuneful South African accent, not the sort that you can cut with a knife. His name was still a legend in cricket circles. Throughout the years from around 1905 to 1914, he had been without question South Africa's finest all-rounder, with a total of 25 Test Match appearances for his country. Some would claim – and with a good deal of substance – that in his time he was the best all-rounder of his age. He was one of South Africa's famous bowling trio: Faulkner, Vogler and Schwarz. All three of them bowled the 'googly' at will, and they caused some havoc among top-class opposition. The man remains vividly in my memory, but I must look to my trusty *Wisdens* for the record.

Faulkner made his final Test appearance for South Africa in that 1924 match at Lords, recalled for just the one game, which England won overwhelmingly. He made 25 and 12, and did not take a wicket. However, he had been one of the match-winners at Eastbourne in 1921 playing for A.C. Maclaren's personally picked England XI, when the all-conquering Australians met one of their two end-of-tour defeats. Faulkner made 3 and 153, and took 6 wickets in the match.

He spent at least some of the Boer War years from 1889 to 1902 in Cape Province, where he would have been in close touch with the British, and where he evidently received his cricket baptism. But I remember being told that he was much affected by the devastation resulting from that unhappy conflict.

The same acquaintance told me that it was with the South African Division at Delville Wood, during the 1916 Somme offensive, that he won his DSO. He finished the Great War with the rank of Major. And now I come to think of it, I don't believe I ever saw Faulkner laugh or even smile.

Sadly, he was to die by his own hand in 1930, soon after I came to know him.

It was at this time, too, that Norman Whitley said

something I've never forgotten. Large, bluff and hearty, he had a considerable stock of wisdom. Having tried to encourage me about my future, his words went something like this:

'I suppose we are all ambassadors in our own small way, and perhaps that's why I like cricket and cricketers.'

It came out quite naturally and unportentously, though in cold print it sounds a bit philosophical for the average pavilion bar. He added something to the effect we were all going to have to learn to be more international in our outlook as the world became smaller and travel became ever quicker and more accessible to millions of people.

Words of uncanny perception, when one remembers how in those far off days, only a privileged few ever so much as contemplated a foreign holiday.

I doubt whether I ever came anywhere near Whitley's standard but I have tried with a capital 'T'. It was from Whitley also that I first heard about evolution. I don't mean the Darwinian sort, which went back into the mists of time and upon which my father had often lectured me. No, he referred to the latter-day evolution (or perhaps revolution) where mankind, his exploits, his speech, his thoughts, his environment and everything about him are all moving at such an accelerating speed. Whitley was eloquent about all this, and I have thought on it quite a bit during these many intervening years.

During this jobless period, I caught up with some of the friends I had left behind four years earlier. I found that still, during their sacred lunch hour, they met and talked almost exclusively about current sporting events. At this time of year it was inevitably rugger that preoccupied them, and their great concern was what might happen to England when 'Wakers' retired. Nothing seemed to have changed. At least they all had jobs and I hadn't. They showed no interest whatever in where I'd been or what I had been doing, and somehow I didn't particularly want to talk about it; our lives had diverged, and only one matter of common interest seemed to remain – where we could get the best possible lunch at the cheapest price.

In those days there was quite a choice: Lyons first and foremost, then the ABC, Express Dairy, and any number of good pubs vying for custom.

London was especially well catered for; you could get coffee and a snack very reasonably indeed, surrounded by other lunchers talking, making play with secretaries, and often indulging the latest craze, dominoes, at marble-topped tables.

If you were prepared to engage in wild expenditure, you could go to Wilkinsons where, for half a crown, you could feast on a roast and two vegetables plus an apple pudding, with coffee thrown in.

The prosperous – and there seemed to be plenty of them at that low ebb in the nation's economic life – shunned such places. The watering holes of the very rich remained as exclusive as ever, but if you had a slightly elevated position in the business world you could enjoy your much longer lunch 'hour' at the London Tavern, or Pymm's.

Somehow, my attitudes seemed out of tune with the times, and I must say I found it all a bit apathetic, in fact very depressing.

Come what may, I was determined to go to any lengths to escape this sort of life, and Bill Galvin agreed with me. But how to do it? Funds were running low, and one of our Malayan friends had gone off to Scotland to try and rear chickens, which seemed to be a risky venture on his tiny capital, and we never heard how he got on.

In the Long Bar at the Troc, we were making half a pint go further than was our normal wont. Bill, sipping morosely at his beer one evening, said, 'What about the Foreign Legion?'

I thought that was a bit too drastic. We agreed that, if the worst came to the worst, we might enlist in one of the Services.

A tower of strength at that time was Sybil, a school friend of my sister. She worked as a receptionist to a Harley Street medical specialist and, as I remember, she was always impeccably turned out. She had a car, very unusual in those days, and she gave the impression of being rich and confident. On some weekends we would go to the Sussex Downs, park the car and walk for long distances, when I would open my heart to her. She was a sympathetic listener.

Once we danced at the Metropole Hotel in Brighton, for which I'm sure she must have paid, and there, in a corner with a woman friend, was Frank Hill, my late Singapore director. We had a very pleasant talk, and he eyed Sybil approvingly. He said, 'I feel certain that you will make out.' Sybil discussed with me my prospects and my desire to travel, but she was destined to die young, far too young. She was a most exceptional girl, whose personality was to stay with me for a while.

Then, one evening in the Long Bar I met a large, fat man, who turned out to be Douglas V. Duff, an adventurer and author of several entertaining books of fiction.

He had served in the Palestine Police and was full of stories about life in that Force. It was Duff who pointed the way towards what was to be my new way of life. The Crown Agents were actively recruiting.

'Eleven pounds per month and everything found' was the offer. 'If you're found medically fit, you could join a draft leaving within a few days.'

I was accepted, and before I could say my farewells satisfactorily I was sailing out of Southampton on the SS *Largs Bay*.

Bill, and the other two ex-Malayan rubber planters who formed our jobless coterie, were to follow a month later. The contract was for two years, and the future after that would have to look after itself. We had been jobless for at least six months. Apart from the generosity and forbearance of my family and the kindnesses of people like Norman Whitley and Sybil, it had seemed a melancholy eternity. Now the trumpets were sounding again and red blood was coursing.

Once more I pulled out on the 'Long Trail, the trail that is always new.'

9

Mount Scopus

It was about 9 a.m. on a May morning in 1932. My six companions and I, with our humble belongings, were decanted from the Morris tender in front of the guard room at the police depot on Mount Scopus, about two miles from Jerusalem at the northern end of the Mount of Olives ridge.

It had been a sleepless and tiring journey by night train up from El Kantara on the Canal. The train snaked along the seaward edge of the Sinai up to Lydda, where we changed to the local train that had climbed up through the Judean hills to Jerusalem.

Bleary-eyed and still covered with the dust that had seeped in everywhere, we stood for a moment and surveyed the scene.

A busy, dusty and already sun-drenched drill square surrounded by wooden huts stretched before us. Squads were drilling everywhere, and bellowed words of command informed us at once of our own fate, from which there was no retreat.

Everybody was wearing a Wolseley pith helmet, a blue collarless shirt, black belt, khaki shorts, blue puttees and black boots. And everyone except us shone brightly.

A corporal who seemed to have inherited us looked long and hard; and showing little enthusiasm, said, 'Christ!' and 'Come with me.'

The rest of the morning, following a breakfast of rissoles,

which I couldn't eat on account of some unprintable comments from the cook, was as busy as I can ever remember.

We drew kit and immediately were shown how to fold and stack it on the kit racks above our beds. A frame was produced, and the folded greatcoat and other items had to fit within it. The frame was then removed and one had to memorize dimensions. New boots (two pairs) sat on either side of the stacked kit. Rifles had to be handcuffed to beds. Bandolier and belt were hung below the rack. An oblong black box was supplied to each of us for storing our civilian kit.

'Sailor' Oliver, one of our number, an extremely handsome man, was in his element. In fact, he'd never had anything to do with the sea; he'd been in the Royal Horse Artillery in India, been 'busted' from sergeant to bombadier, left the army and passed through many an adventurous hoop. For a few weeks before enlisting in the Palestine Police, he'd been on his uppers, sleeping either rough or in Rowton Houses when he could afford them. He'd embarked with us on the SS *Largs Bay* without a 'nicker', and I had in fact lent him £10 of my remaining £30 to help him through.

Sailor returned the loan as soon as he was able. Now that we were raw recruits on 'Scopus' he repaid the gesture by helping us to adjust with his own street wisdom.

He knew the ropes and saw to it that we understood them. We were indeed lucky to have him as our mentor. He showed us how to get rid of the grease on boots, belt and bandolier, and how to make them shine like glass.

It was of course a long and arduous process, but at least we learnt quickly, and he lectured us on the sanctity of the rifle, with lurid details of the kind of thing that happened on the North-West Frontier of India.

Our corporal, whose duty it would normally have been to give us this kind of introductory rundown, thankfully left us in Sailor's capable charge.

We were surrounded with history, though nobody seemed to be much bothered by that fact.

Here it was in 70 AD that the Roman General Titus, later to don the 'Purple' in succession to his father Vespasian, was to marshall his Legions - the 5th, the 10th, the 12th and the 15th - for the final assault on the insurgents in Jewish-held Jerusalem. It was said that he who held the Antonia Fortress held the key to the Temple; and he who held the Temple held the key to Jerusalem. And it was upon the Antonia that the might of the Legions fell.

It was very near to the police depot that Titus, reconnoitring close to the City walls down in the Kedron valley, was surprised by a sortie of Jewish soldiers from within that grim 60-feet-high city boundary.

It must have been on our second or third morning that I was given an introduction to 'Tickatty', who was a senior camp lavatory attendant and odd job man - our Gunga Din.

I had just met Norman Lash, who was in a squad senior to us, and he and I had struck an accord. Lash, later to become Glubb Pasha's second-in-command in the Arab Legion, was a Tonbridgian and an Oxford graduate. Caught up in the economic slump, like so many of us, he'd been glad to enlist in the Palestine Police. He was always laughing, and his wit was infectious.

He and I were walking away from the Mess hut one day when he espied a diminutive figure in a battered trilby hat and called to him with solemn formality.

'Mr Tickatty, permit me to introduce a newcomer in our midst, Mr Imray. I feel sure that you will accord him all assistance within your particular sphere.'

'Yes, sah,' said Tickatty, doffing his tatty old hat, 'pleased to meet any friend of Mr Lash. Not too bad here, is it Sah?'

Guard duty was routine from the outset at Scopus. The guard was mounted at 6 p.m. amd dismounted at 6 a.m. the following day. It was a matter of two hours on duty and four hours off. The Guard Commander read out the Orders, which included action to be taken in the event of fire.

On my first tour of duty the Guard Commander was A.L. Alexander, then on a corporal's promotional course. In much later years he was to become the last European police chief in the Gold Coast before, as an independent republic it became Ghana. On this occasion I had paid insufficient attention to our briefing, and at 2 a.m., while I was wandering around the camp, we were visited by the OC Depot, Major Munroe.

'What are your fire orders?' he asked as I slapped my rifle butt in salute.

I stammered but didn't know. The next day I was 'up the hill' on a charge, and so – separately – was poor Alexander. We were both given three extra guard duties.

I learnt to opt for the unpopular 4-6 a.m. shift because at a certain point on my beat I could watch the sun rise over the hills of Moab and then inflame in a glory of red and gold the domes and spires and minarets of Jerusalem's Old City.

We were not permitted to remove our boots when off-duty in the guardroom. I recall an occasion when my feet were hurting and I did remove mine. At that unlucky juncture we were visited by an inspecting officer who turned out the guard.

I could never have hoped to get away with it and in my violent rush to turn out, I failed to note a scorpion in one of my boots, and I got stung. It was a most unpleasant business, and I had no sympathy from anyone – and probably deserved none. In due course I was once more 'up the hill' on a charge.

Cricketwise, this trip lacked the *laissez faire* atmosphere, the breezy quality of makeshift fixtures and spontaneous fun that we had found in the backblocks of Malaysia. It was serious stuff.

Early in my time at Scopus, all the 40 to 50 new recruits were summoned to the sports ground. Our chief, the forceful, dedicated Inspector-General, R.G.B. Spicer, was a man to whom cricket was little short of a religion.

He duly arrived amid much pomp and ceremony, dressed not in the uniform of Police Commissioner but in cricket apparel. He was wearing – if I remember correctly – a Free Foresters' cap.

Bidden to circle round him, we were addressed thus: 'It is essential that the force has a cricket team of which we can all be proud – yes, essential.' He had a habit of underlining his main clauses as if he was writing them into a police report.

'Cricket is part of our British tradition, and as such it must be played in the proper spirit. You must understand this – yes, understand it.'

There was much more in the same vein; it might just as well have been A.K., Sniffy Clark or Aubrey Wallich talking.

We were then put through our paces in the nets and eventually reduced to a mere 15 or so who, in R.G.B.s very expert opinion, were 'possibilities'. Most were dismissed out of hand; they hadn't wanted to be with us in the first place and declared emphatically, though not within the hearing of R.G.B., that they neither knew nor cared which end of a bat to hold.

R.G.B. believed implicitly in cricket as the *sine qua non* of character formation. With Lord Harris, he saw the game not merely as sport but as a 'moral lesson'. Rather like Sniffy, he did not entirely trust men who failed to understand its subtleties.

I can still feel the magnetic, compulsive power of this man of small physical stature, of patent quality of leadership, and indeed of ruthlessness when he was required to be tough. 'This man is out' would be his verdict on anyone who deliberately transgressed the rules or failed through lack of effort to measure up to his standards; who, in short, 'let the side down'. His own credentials were impressive enough.

At St Paul's School, Roy Godfrey Bullen Spicer had been captain of cricket and boxing, and he won a scholarship place at Balliol. He was, incidentally, a school contemporary of Montgomery, and the approaches of the two men to work and play always seemed to me to have much in common. He served his police cadetship in Ceylon under Sir Herbert Dowbiggin before joining the Carabiniers in the 1914-18 war, being seriously wounded and badly gassed in France, and winning the MC. He went on to command the Kenya police force before, in 1931, being appointed Inspector-General in Palestine.

It was R.G.B. who, over the years, was to forge a cricket XI that became second to none in the Middle East. Indeed after I left Palestine in 1935 the police were able to produce two XIs of almost equal calibre. Even in my own time, during the formative period of the Palestine Police CC, an excellent standard was reached.

Early in my time, it would have been sometime in 1933, we of the Force XI were to play a Middle East Services team up in Amman, the capital city of the country that was then called Trans-Jordan (now Jordan).

Having crossed Allenby Bridge over the Jordan river in police tenders, we were climbing up towards the heights where lay Amman when there was a crackle of musketry and one of our number was left cursing fluently, with a slug embedded in his arm.

We had been ambushed, luckily without serious consequence. Our escort blazed off into the 'blue', but the pattern was one that many Palestine policemen came to know over the years. Those rocky Jordanian hillsides provided perfect cover for bandits.

Despite this small mishap, we arrived at our rendezvous on the RAF landing ground at Amman, where I and another inquisitive member of the party strolled to look at an aircraft some 200 yards away. We got into desultory conversation with an aircraftsman working on a wing tip. After some 20 minutes of this idle chatter, something jogged my memory and I looked hard at the aircraftsman. He was older than us and had a long lantern-jawed face. He smiled a lot, but was not exactly chatty. There was no doubt in my mind that in appearance he was very like the photographs of T.E. Lawrence that we had all become aware of following the publication of *The Seven Pillars of Wisdom,* and the post-war lectures of the American Lowell Thomas. He accompanied us to the RAF Sergeants' Mess, where he vanished, and we rejoined our party.

I made an enquiry and was told that our friend had only been about a week in Amman, and yes - the very close likeness to T.E. Lawrence had been noted, but he was quartered separately and nobody had spoken more than a few words to him.

My subsequent enquiries suggested that the enigmatic Lawrence, according to available records, should then have been either up on the North-West Frontier of India, or else at Calshott in Britain. Had we come across some new sidelight on his movements, or were we imagining the likeness?

I couldn't believe my eyes. I had just come off guard duty at Scopus and - bless my soul ' who was that long angular figure with the drooping moustache? There was no mistake. It was 'Bloody' Matthews, unseen and unheard of since Kuala Lumpur, when we both received our marching orders.

Matthews was surveying the Square with a thoroughly jaundiced eye.

'To think it should come to bloody this,' he observed succinctly. I couldn't help agreeing. He was certainly the last person I would have expected to find in police uniform. Anyway, I took him in hand as best I could and introduced him to another Matthews, Doug Matthews, who was our camp cook. Matthews and the rest of the intake of recruits were 'brigaded' with our squad for drill purposes, in the military jargon that governed our lives, despite the constant insistence of R.G.B. that we were essentially 'civilians in uniform'.

There are some people who seem constitutionally incapable of marching properly. They can walk with perfect normality, but on a barrack square they are lost. They get into a terrible muddle, with left leg and left arm swinging in unison, and right leg and arm ditto. The result is always grotesque. Just such a one was 'Bloody' Matthews.

There was a dreadful morning on the square when we were marching up and down, with the corporal vainly trying to get Matthews to march properly. Then he (the corporal) roared 'About turn,' which everybody accomplished except Matthews, who had been left-hand file and was now doing a kind of goose step on his own over towards one of the huts. Eventually he was brought up sharp against a wall and was marking time in a most peculiar fashion, unaware that he was on his own.

He might well have carried on doing this for ever, but the corporal marched us behind Matthews and made his way ominously towards the offending recruit.

The corporal whispered in his ear, 'Didn't you hear me give the command' – his voice rose to a scream – 'About turn?' He then turned and faced us, threw his stick on the ground, jumped on it and declared, 'And now we know why rabbits scoff their young.'

It was certainly a baptism of fire for poor Matthews, and there came a time when in an unguarded moment he allowed the corporal to hear him emit a *sotto voce* 'Bloody hell.' The result was inevitable: punishment drill – circumnavigating the square at the double with his rifle at the high port.

Matthews's marching was eventually brought under control by Sailor Oliver, who took him in hand and had him going up and down the barrack room with the rest of us singing some awful song; and at long last we had him marching normally. But all was not well.

Matthews was very proud of his luxuriant drooping moustache, but somebody cut off the two ends while he was asleep. Even in the liberated atmosphere of the late 20th century, I forbear to record my ex-boss's words when he saw himself in the mirror.

Those early weeks at Scopus were rough and ready. Sunday was a day off and the seashore at Tel Aviv was attractive. Some of our recruits had no idea of the power of the Middle

East sun, and after a day on the beach they were badly burnt.

Head Constable Black addressed us on parade next day: 'I hear that some of you young men like the sun. I get all the sun I need up here on Mount Scopus, and so, I promise, will you.'

With that the squad instrutors took perverse delight in doubling us round the square with our rifles at the slope, frequently changing shoulder. By the end of a session, shoulders were very raw and two recruits were taken to hospital 'Human rights' was not an acknowledged thesis in those days.

Our drill instructors were all ex-Guardsmen, and the Guards tradition at that time was first to break a recruit so that later he could be turned into a trained soldier.

Our three months' training period was not entirely devoted to 'square-bashing', plus the inevitable 6.30 a.m. physical training. There was an extensive programme of lectures and note-taking on elementary law, first aid, and almost every aspect of police procedure as it applied to Palestine. There was indeed a most detailed Police Manual, which one was expected to learn by heart. A complete knowledge of the Manual was essential before one could be considered for promotion to the exalted rank of Corporal.

Also at Scopus in my time, though I believe the practice was later discontinued, an attempt was made to teach several methods of self-defence, in those days known by the blanket title of *Ju-jitsu.*

An early visitor to our hut - or rather to Sailor in particular - was from a more senior squad. He was called 'Burglar' Burton, and had been in the Royals. Legend had it that one of his mates in the Royals was to be court-martialed, and Burton had broken into the Adjutant's office at night and removed certain incriminating evidence that would have convicted his pal. Thus he was dubbed 'Burglar', and the name stuck.

One day a warrant was received at Scopus from France,

where Sailor had worked for a while as a chauffeur, seeking his extradition on a criminal charge. Sailor, who had already made his mark at Scopus and was highly popular, was consigned for a short while to the grim fortress of Acre. A deep gloom settled over everybody. Investigations were accelerated, and it was found that the charge against Sailor could not possibly be sustained. Proceedings were dropped by the French authorities, to whom an officer of the Palestine Government had been sent for face-to-face talks, and Sailor returned to a riotous welcome at Scopus. Everybody wanted to buy him a celebratory drink.

The British Section of the Palestine Police Force was a great 'leveller'. Within our ranks we had all kinds, from the high to the low and humbly born; indeed, some liked to refer to us – with doubtful accuracy – as the British Foreign Legion.

Nevertheless, there were inevitable cliques which sometimes took on a 'class' complexion, if only because in every society Like tends to gravitate to Like.

I have told before the tale of how R.G.B. and cricket were inextricably linked, and how they came to play a joint and decisive part in my life and progress in the Palestine force. From those who are familiar with the earlier version*, I must ask forgiveness for the sin of repetition.

My earliest memory of R.G.B. is of a parade at HQ soon after our arrival. We lined up outside his office and were shown in one at a time. Spicer, physically a small compact figure, sat at a large desk, with another officer, Michael O'Rorke (of three-pip status) alongside him. I had the impression that R.G.B. had me summed up straight away.

Was I bent on a career in the force, or was I simply waiting for something better to turn up?

'I expect a truthful answer,' he insisted.

I wanted to make a career in the force, I told him.

---

* *Policeman in Palestine.*

'Good. At school at Malvern, I see. Played cricket there, I suppose.'

Fortunately he didn't wait for me to reply, since I had failed to make the School XI.

'Where did you bat?'

I replied somewhat equivocally that I usually batted in the top half of the order, 'Usually three to five, Sir.'

'Fine. Bowl at all?'

'Yes, Sir, right arm, Sir, off-breaks.'

'Any good at boxing?'

'No, Sir.'

'Pity. That's all, Imray. I shall expect to see you at cricket nets. O'Rorke, kindly make sure that Sergeant Alderson shows Imray the ropes.'

I have told already of the first encounter with him at nets. What I neglected to say was that on that occasion, after R.G.B. had dealt severely with the recruits' bowling, I pitched a ball several inches outside his stumps and flicked his off bail. He looked intently at the point where the ball landed, followed its trajectory with the bat, and said, 'Well bowled, young man.'

Soon afterwards names went on the notice board for that first game against the Combined Forces XI in Amman, when we met Lawrence or his double at the airfield. I was delighted, of course, to find myself included.

Bill Wainwright, very much my senior as District 'Super' in Jerusalem, was an agreeable colleague in the early games, and we were lucky with the intake of recruits both to the ranks and the officer echelons. Laurie Harrington, also a 'Super', was a good cricketer, and even better was H.S. Swain, an Assistant Super who came from Kenya and had played for Gloucester.

There was only one drawback to Scopus cricket, the playing field. It was hard, bumpy and bare, and despite R.G.B.'s artful use of working parties and punishment squads to bring it up to scratch, ground fielding was always a dicey affair.

There was a very unfortunate mix-up in one of the

important early matches – I can't be sure, but I think it was against an RAF XI. I came in at number four or five to join R.G.B. who was scoring well, and after one or two balls, called him for a quick single. I hesitated, and when he was several paces up the wicket I realized we weren't going to make it, and called out, 'Go back.' But it was too late. It was all my fault, and R.G.B. simply kept on running past the broken wicket and into the pavilion.

What a brilliant move! I had foolishly run out my skipper and my commanding officer who had quite a few runs under his belt. I trembled at the crease as I tried to make amends with a few runs of my own. In fact, I accumulated a reasonable score before departing. I approached the pavilion with some foreboding. And there, to my relief, was R.G.B. to welcome me in with a modest handclap. 'Well played Imray,' was all he said.

Later, seeing that I was still uneasy, he said, 'Don't worry, lad, it happens to all of us.'

Spicer was a most knowledgeable and inspiring captain. He seemed off the field to know everyone who was anyone in the world of cricket. I once heard him talking to A.C. Maclaren's brother and, imagining that pearls of cricket wisdom flowed, I inclined an ear. R.G.B. was telling him all about his police training methods.

On the field he was full of enthusiasm, sometimes a bit too much so for our star fast bowler, 'Chinny' Fletcher. R.G.B. had the habit of changing the field just slightly every time one of Chinny's deliveries went past the bat or veered away from the off stump, perhaps taking out a slip or moving cover point or gully a few inches with the result that a catch that would almost certainly have gone to hand the ball before would find the boundary, and Chinny would go back to his mark with the hang-dog look of a man whose best laid plans had been bitched by well-meant interference.

Incidentally, I remember that R.G.B. used to say that Chinny was as fast as E.A. McDonald, the Australian Test bowler.

We soon became far too good for most of the local

opposition, and through R.G.B.'s influence we began to find fixtures all over the Near East.

There were some close encounters with powerful Army and Navy sides from Cairo and Alexandria, and return fixtures were eagerly arranged. We defeated the Middlesex Regiment by the narrowest of margins after their main bowler, Kennett, went through us with alarming rapidity. I was top scorer with 18 and took four wickets, and thanks to Chinny's support they ended up two or three runs short of our total. On another occasion, I won the praise of R.G.B. for a stoical innings which lasted an hour and a half and brought forth six runs, thus forcing a draw against the Grenadiers.

We very nearly had to eat humble pie against the Nazareth Divisional side. Two of their bowlers, Stacey Barham and Bob Jarrett were devastating on a bumpy wicket and, if I remember correctly, had us all out for under 50. Fortunately, Chinny Fletcher responded with one of his lethal spells, and we won by a run or two.

Then Hubert Ashton* appeared at Jerusalem on a visit. It was poor Chinny's moment of truth.

In *Wisden* it was written that during the 1921 season, when England in their own land, were outclassed by Australia, Ashton - then a Cambridge Blue at cricket, soccer and hockey - was one of the few English batsmen who played with any confidence against the two Australian fast bowlers, Gregory and MacDonald. Yet he never played in a Test Match. In the one match in which he played against us, Ashton hit our prize bowler all over the place.

In fact, the opposition seemed to grow in unison with us. There were often some fine cricketers among the garrison, though a good many were simply passing through - A.J.H. (Jim) Cassells of the Seaforths, for example, who had a meteoric army career and finished as a Field Marshal and CIGS.

---

* Later Sir Hubert Ashton, KBE, MC.

Other well-remembered names that spring to mind are Squadron Leader Steel and Sergeant Monk of the RAF, and Captain (later General) Alexander of the Gordons. There was also an outstanding medium-pace spin bowler named Monks who returned to England to play in the Lancashire league.

This was a time too, when powerful cricket teams went on tour, and in my time we had men playing against us of the ilk of R.W.V. Robins and Ian Peebles.

As for our Police team, the formidable Fletcher was supported by Swain and Johnson, two able medium-pacers, wrist-spinners Woolnough and Marvin, with myself to provide off-spin when all else failed and Penry Price, who bowled what would nowadays count as seamers. There was another excellent fast bowler who played only occasionally, and whose sporting career came to an abrupt end when he was stabbed in the Jaffa riots in 1933.

As for batting, we opened with Good and Viall, who seldom failed to give us a respectable start to the innings; and the latter read Peebles well when that redoubtable cricketer came to Jerusalem with a touring side. R.G.B. generally came in at number three, followed by Swain, Price, Frank Macadam and myself. 'Tiger' Watson and Jim Imrie were our keepers; R.G.B. had some difficulty in deciding between them, thought Imrie was sometimes selected for his 'agricultural' batting when it was felt that a do-or-die innings might be called for.

There it was. Not all the people I have named made more than a ripple on the surface of the game. I name them all because, in the context of that time in mandated Palestine, where Britain inherited the conscience of the Western world and tried to keep the peace between indigenous Arab and world Jewry, between Judaism, Christianity and Islam, they – we – carried on our game in its true tradition, welcoming to our ranks anyone who was prepared to understand the axioms involved, that it is a game governed not by rules but by laws, that winning within the law is the prior aim, and cheating an unforgivable sin.

The Palestine Police were a motley crew. We had with us an Irish Peer*, an ex-coal miner, and a Billingagate fish porter; in fact just about every calling in life, legitimate and otherwise.

It was a strict, but friendly regime, but there was one misfit: a very able recruit who was soon in line for promotion. He was made up to Corporal, and it was widely believed that he would be the first recruit ever to be commissioned from the ranks.

But there was a curious racist element in his make-up. We all knew it, but R.G.B., who took pride in the international attitude of his team, evidently did not. Our Corporal flatly refused to salute an Arab officer, and this, of course, was the end for him. He was on the boat home in no time at all. The Arab officer, to his credit, had remained silent.

It was a blow to our pride. Contrary to a belief that has grown up since those formative years, our Palestine comrades - Arab and Jew - were an integral and vital part of the force, and though there was rivalry, there was no lack of respect, generally speaking, on one side or another.

If there was no room for exclusivity at Scopus, there was one 'untouchable' group, a self-appointed élite. These were the veterans from Ireland, and they numbered among them both Republicans and 'Black and Tans'. They sat together in the canteen, perhaps telling of their past exploits with no shadow of hostility. Perhaps they had deep and dark secrets. It was, whatever the reasons, a company to which outsiders were never admitted.

We had an Arab officer, who was greatly respected, by the name of Abdin. He was my superior officer, but I looked upon him also as a friend; he certainly had a superb sense of humour.

I remember being invited to join him one evening in Jerusalem's Vienna cafe. I was there with my friend Bill Galvin, and Abdin asked us about 'this cricket'. What was it about this strange ritual, he wanted to know, that our

* Pat Wingfield, 9th Baron Powerscourt

Inspector-General was so keen about? I tried to explain, while Bill kept silent. It took me a long time, and at the end of my dissertation Abdin decided that he would not make a cricketer.

Then our host asked Bill, 'Do you too play cricket?'

'No, Sir, I play rugger.'

'Could I play this rugger?'

'No, Sir. With respect, you are too fat.'

Abdin's familiar roar of laughter rang across Zion Square, as it did on many a night.

There lived and worked in Palestine a brand of people who were very different from the usual types of Colonials whom I was to meet in both West and East Africa.

The Palestine climate was good, and non-indigneous people of all races lived there because they had come under the country's spell, and because in their own particular trade or calling there was plenty of work for them to do, with side interests of all kinds. There were archaeologists and a thriving intelligensia, imported and indigenous, at the heart of which was an outstanding American who, through a chance meeting, became a close friend. He was Edward C. Blatchford, a wealthy bachelor who had made his home in Palestine, living in a very well-appointed flat close to the King David Hotel in Jerusalem. Blatchford had been around in the Middle East since before World War One, and he was extremely knowledgeable about historical and contemporary matters.

Blatchford struck up a close friendship with Abdin Bey, and there were many others who gathered at his flat - especially on a Sunday afternoon - to consume tea and rock cakes dispensed by his factotum, Eissa. In Blatchford's company, Palestine and its people, its history and everything about it, came alive.

When my tour of duty in Palestine ended and I was gazetted to officer status and bidden to Africa, I was taken to Jerusalem's railway station by Edward Blatchford in his ancient car, driven by Eissa. My friend said he had long forgotten how to drive, and had never been very good at it anyway.

At the station we ran into 'Bloody' Matthews who, with one other, had been there on duty all night. He gave Blatchford an excellent salute and then turned to me with a farewell handshake.

But he couldn't resist a final Matthews diatribe. Somebody had evidently forgotten to send the tender to collect him. 'Bloody transport,' he said. 'Leave you in the bloody lurch. Typical.'

It was not quite the last time I was to see Matthews.

Blatchford, a truly cosmopolitan American who had been a cowboy in his time, bade him farewell and then, as he off-loaded me, he asked, 'Did anyone ever try to teach Matthews to play cricket?'

10

The 'Mad Hatter'

I arrived at Accra on the Gold Coast in June 1935, with boundless pride in my recent elevation from the police ranks and, I must confess, with almost boundless regard for the people whom I had just left in Palestine.

There in Palestine was an international community of non-indigenous peoples who had until very recent times lived contentedly alongside their Arab neighbours, and who displayed an abiding interest in the country which they shared.

And if the amity that had existed under the centuries of Ottoman Turkish rule had begun to break up, it seemed to me, nevertheless, to stand in virtuous contrast to the indifference of Gold Coast expatriates to the country they had come to dominate.

There were, of course, notable exceptions, in administrative ranks especially, but there was always in my experience a feeling of impermanence.

Then came the Second World War, and almost overnight the picture seemed to change. New organizations sprouted, bringing new people and fresh ideas in train. Pan American Airways, soon to merge with the American Army Air Corps, came to Accra, and we were inundated with Americans, who basked in the sun while we Europeans hid ourselves from its rays with all kinds of elaborate protective devices.

They revolutionized our way of thinking, and soon we were following their example and wallowing in the sun's warmth and proudly displaying our bronzed bodies.

Two battalions of troops, comprising the Gold Coast Regiment, were heavily expanded, and a large number of white Rhodesians were imported to provide an adequate cadre of officers and NCOs. The Gold Coast Regiment, brigaded with large units from Nigeria, Sierra Leone and the Gambia, was to achieve a lasting reputation in the East African and Burma campaigns. The old conservatism of a rather complacent expatriate population gave way all of a sudden to a lively, cosmopolitan atmosphere.

But what of the Gold Coast Africans themselves? How typically do we leave them till last. But inevitably they were the last people a white newcomer got to know, and from the outset I found them a very different proposition. They appealed to me greatly; indeed, I can say that, by and large, they were the most attractive African people that I have met anywhere in that vast continent.

They had a laughing lifestyle; they were usually good-mannered, and they were exuberant and colourful in all that they did. Their sense of humour was remarkably 'English' and delightfully unsophisticated.

I have to say that I did find the people of Ashanti – that vast rain-forested area of the country – somewhat silent and difficult to communicate with, unlike the native population elsewhere; but they were the exception.

Along the coastline the people had been in contact for several hundred years with the West, and had been at the mercy not only of the infamous slave traders, but also of the warlike Ashanti warriors from the interior.

I was to come under the aegis of two Colonial Governors, Sir Arnold Hodson and Sir Alan Burns. The latter succeeded in 1941, and his Governorship lasted until 1947.

I was to meet Burns not only in the Gold Coast, but on several occasions in Britain, after his retirement and right up to near the end of his long life. Every now and again when I was in England he would ask me to lunch at the Athenaeum, and anyone who knew him will guess that cricket figured large in our conversation.

Never more than a middle-rank cricketer of average club standard, I had my moments of inspiration - which every average sportsman will recognize - when to universal astonishment, including my own, everything went right for me and I seemed to be able to do no wrong. I appeared on those occasions to be a far better player than in fact I was. The result of this unpredictability was that I was sometimes picked to play at a level higher than my ability warranted.

But - and this too will be familiar to most players in and outside the ranks of the first-class game - the better the company, the better I played.

Thus I arrived in the Gold Coast with a cricket reputation which followed me from Palestine; I think that my late chief, R.G.B. had been over-kind to me in his appraisal of my cricket. Anyway, deserved or not, this reputation was considerably enhanced when in my first game for an Accra team against a local African XI, I made a century in uncharacteristically cavalier fashion.

I doubt, to tell the truth, whether the bowling in that particular game was very formidable, although African cricket in the Gold Coast at that time was by no means negligible.

Football suited the exuberant and extrovert Gold Coast character better than did cricket, but there were some fine cricketers around. When in full flow they had the panache that is so familiar in the batting of the West Indians; and they had among them some very useful bowlers, whilst their fielding was always keen and acrobatic. I always thought that a properly managed Gold Coast team, bolstered up by one or two local Indians, many of whom were spin bowlers of real class and most of whom had clearly batted before, would have been very formidable.

One evening I asked three African cricketers to come and have a drink at my bungalow. I had also asked John Hooton, a brilliant policeman-turned-senior legal man, whom I had known in Palestine and who turned up in Accra at much the same time as myself. Inevitably we talked cricket, and one of the long-suffering Africans asked with studied politeness what we were talking about. I – being well into my second large Scotch – launched into a diatribe on cricket and its history, recalling my experiences with people like A.K., Sniffy Clark and Aubrey Wallich, and going on at great length about the game's great ones such as 'W.G.', Hobbs and Bradman, then at the height of his fame. Increasingly in my cups, I told the uncomprehending audience about the occasion on which my infant head was patted by W.G. –thus becoming a protégé of the great man? John, himself a non-believer as far as cricket was concerned, was bursting at the seams with amusement, not at my story but at the faces of the black listeners.

There was an annual home-and-away test match between the Gold Coast and Nigeria, which took place in Accra and Lagos. In those days, of course, the teams consisted of Europeans only. The big occasion was looming, and it seemed that I was a candidate for selection after my auspicious beginning.

But my form fell away, and not until much later on did I regain it. I was not picked to represent the Colony, and I had to watch from a rickety shed that passed for the members' stand at Accra.

From memory I would think that at least two Africans would have improved the team from the Gold Coast, which usually lost its one international fixture. There were some good European cricketers around in both Colonies; some of them were university Blues who had played the odd game for their counties.

The Accra 'Oval' was not an inviting cricket arena. It consisted of a large expanse of reddish-brown laterite without a blade of grass anywhere, and upon this, in the middle, was stretched a matting wicket.

The outfield was marginally better than it was at our police cricket gound at Mount Scopus in Palestine, where we had to contend with rocks and stones that were eternally pushing their way to the surface and causing a fielder quite a few problems. R.G.B. had been heard to say that if a man could field really well at Scopus, he was worth his place in any side.

But to play cricket in the very humid West African climate in not very attractive surroundings, one needed to be very much an enthusiast.

At Accra, moreover, nobody had ever been able to find the money, or perhaps the energy, to provide an even passable pavilion. All we had was a shack with a verandah and an inside room where one could change. There was at this time no wash basin nor even a lavatory, and the whole edifice badly needed repairs and a coat of paint. Yet this was the venue for the inter-Colonial 'Test Match'.

Kumasi, I recall, was better off. The cricket arena was of coarse grass which was at least green, in the cricket tradition, though once again there was the inevitable matting wicket. I believe, from rather indistinct memory, that the 'pavilion' was in better shape than the Accra monstrosity.

Gold Coast cricket at this time was largely directed by Patrick Fitzgerald, who was a manager of the United Africa Company. He had played some good class cricket in Britain. His headquarters, however, were in Kumasi, 150 miles from Accra, and he was a busy up-and-coming man in his vast company. He was rarely seen in whites; indeed, until the war, there was no outstanding cricket personality. We badly needed an R.G.B. or a Sniffy Clark to put the game on its feet.

The West African climate was very enervating, even along the littoral, where there was frequently a breeze. Up-country and away from the coast, conditions have to be experienced to be believed. I look back with some astonishment that so many of us managed to survive.

West African heat can only be compared to Delhi's 'Inner City', so graphically described by Rudyard Kipling in his immortal story 'The City of Dreadful Night'. I recall certain totally airless occasions when, gasping for air under the essential mosquito net, I wondered whether I would survive until morning. In the Gold Coast by my time, the incidence of yellow fever had been very largely neutralized, but there were still occasional outbreaks, and as late as 1926 the military cantonments at Kintampo in northern Ashanti had to be abandoned after a number of deaths. I well remember the cemetery at Elmina on the coast, where the dates on the gravestones indicated very clearly the ravages of this dread disease in much earlier times, when the Gold Coast lived up to its name – 'The White Man's Grave'.

Malaria was still a plague that was very much to be reckoned with. I had suffered sporadically from it ever since my Malayan days. Mercifully, however, I was to be cured, though I had to wait for my second West African 'tour' in Cape Coast, where I encountered Dr Bermingham, later to become illustrious in medical and health circles. I owe him a debt of gratitude for curing me, and as far as I am aware I was never re-infected.

It was at Cape Coast during that second tour of duty that we essayed some makeshift cricket on a piece of wasteland below the Club.

I've forgotten how it all started. I certainly had nothing to do with it. It could well have been at the instigation of the Reverend Fenby, a Methodist Minister from one of the three big educational establishments in our midst. Not only was he a dedicated cricketer with a strong belief in the game's 'mystic properties', but he was also keen on anything that promoted racial harmony and integration.

The two teams included a lady on each side. Several Africans had been dragooned into playing, somewhat against their own inclinations, if I am not mistaken.

When the appointed day came, it was clear that Fenby was another of our colonial princes of the game who inspire, organize and play with verve, and often with unsuspected natural ability. Again, time has dimmed some of the detail, but I vividly recall the memorable part played by Father Holland, who taught at one or other of our places of education.

I see him clearly across 60 years. There he is, in his white smock with a solar topee, fielding in the covers. The ball is hit high in the air in his direction, and he solemnly removes his hat, holds it in two hands and catches the descending cherry in it, as if that is the customary way of doing it. The batsman protests but is adjudged out by an umpire who, in any case, had been looking the other way.

Then, bless me, he does it again, this time off a sizzling uppish cover drive with much power behind it. Like lightning he whips off his hat, thrusts it out, and the ball sticks.

The victim was heard to mutter something about 'bloody bad manners' as he left the field of play, and the Father was known as the 'Mad Hatter' ever after.

It was all so surprising and picturesque that I see it happening now as if time had not intervened.

After the game, I recall, I bought Father Holland a large gin for his feat and we had a good laugh about his unorthodox fielding, which he said he had perfected at Stonyhurst in the lowest cricketing circles. Years later I was in Lagos and met him walking around on the Marina, looking disconsolate.

'I've just been Nigerianized,' he said. 'They've got a black Bishop, and so I've got to go back home to Ireland.'

'Not much cricket there,' I said.

'You'd be surprised,' he replied. 'In fact,' he added, 'they're astonishingly old-fashioned about the laws; no more catchin' in the bowl of my hat.'

He had always enjoyed his gin and we repaired to the nearest hostelry.

11

Gold Coast Capers

There was another memorable Cape Coast game at that period. It had been organized at my own behest, and was a return match against Sekondi, to be played on the big sports ground in the middle of Cape Coast.

I was thirsting for revenge after a previous defeat in Sekondi, and had organized a team that I thought - apart from two tyros - would do the trick. I had personally supervised the wicket and considered we had it in perfect order. Then, just as the match was about to start, we had our first blow. Our fast bowler, Ken Cowan, upon whom I was relying, as he was a player of some calibre who had represented the Colony against Nigeria, announced that he had 'flu and was going home to bed.

We got going, however, and I was batting and going well. It was one of those days when nothing could go wrong - I felt it in my bones. And then I was proved wrong. I stepped back to cut a good-length one past cover to the boundary when the delivery encountered something that had obtruded under the matting on my 'perfect' wicket. The ball slid straight along the ground and hit middle stump. I've never forgotten it.

The only member of our team to emerge with credit was one of the tyros who, flailing wildly, collected just enough runs for us to avoid total disgrace. We lost the match all the same.

Memories came back of Kuala Krai in Malaya, but

somehow nothing could compare with Malayan cricket or with that crazy period of cricket in the backblocks. In the Gold Coast, and indeed in other parts of Africa, bare fields and matting wickets in sprawling townships could not compare with the steamy pastures of Malaysia, with the almost supernatural influence of Sniffy, Aubrey Wallich and A.K. issuing from some distant valhalla; and there was a distinct absence of *joie de vivre* in my new environment.

Then came war, and cricket, like everything else, was transformed. Among the Rhodesians who now engulfed us were some top-class cricketers, including Dennis Tomlinson, who had toured for South Africa against England in 1935. He had played in one Test.

Somewhat to my surprise, I was included in a Gold Coast XI that played against the Rhodesians, which the Rhodesians won. I can't resist the recollection that I distinguished myself with the bat against some class bowling, particularly from Jack Charsley, who had taken a number of wickets against a near full-strength English touring side. I made 50-plus and was very pleased with myself. It was, after all, the genuine upper-class article.

Bowling in one of our 'better' games, this time against a Combined Services side, I was being carted all over the Accra Oval by a crouching left-hander with a cap worn over one eye. When he got out I said to him, 'You look very like Roy Kilner.' (The great Yorkshire and England all-rounder of the 1920s.) He said, 'I am Roy Kilner.'

It was the great man's son, and the two of them were as like as two peas.

At last our Gold Coast cricket played host to a dominant personality. This was Dr B.B. Waddy, who for some years had been buried alive somewhere up country amid humid heat, and had somehow survived with his vitality unscathed.

B.B. was an Australian with strong convictions on most matters, not least on cricket, who came from a family of some repute in cricketing Australia.

He was assisted in his drive to put Gold Coast cricket into

a better state of repair by C.D.A. ('Plug') Pullan, with whom I had been at school at Malvern. The pair of them brooked no excuses; if you were a cricketer you were expected to play.

I became unpopular for a while, because I had the temerity to get involved in some special police duties and simply hadn't time for anything else. However, I was forgiven in the end.

Plug Pullan had played cricket on a number of occasions for Worcestershire; he was a natural all-round games player and had a boxing Blue. It was unfortunate for both B.B. and Plug that they happened to be 'up' at Oxford when its cricket was very strong indeed, with people of the talents of Alan Melville, the Nawab of Pataudi, N.M. Ford, A.M. Crawley, Ian Peebles and Garland Wells all available to play. Neither B.B. nor Plug achieved their Blues which, had they been able to compete in less exalted company, they must surely have done, as they were both very fine cricketers.

B.B. became a Harlequin, which for a non-Blue was an uncommon honour. He and Plug took command of Accra cricket, and they even brought into our fold several Americans, one of whom became 'hooked' on the game and developed into a very fair performer. African cricketers, too, were given an encouraging boost under that enterprising pair.

Part of my term in this part of Africa was spent in the Northern Territories, a vast segment of the country consisting of low bush between the rain forests of Ashanti and the fringes of the southern Sahara deserts. As luck would have it, B.B. spent a while in the same area.

There were some 15 or so 'stations' spread around this block - most of them along the line of the French colonial frontier by which we were surrounded. Distances were considerable, and the administrative officers who ran the districts led very isolated and solitary lives.

But there was a 'frontier' split among these officers. There was always competition in the Gold Coast administrative service for a posting to the NTs (Northern Territories), as they were called.

For me, as a police officer, it was a plum job, though not – I think – regarded at police headquarters as being a particularly important command. It lasted me for some 12 months, and in some ways it was the happiest time of my entire service, even though it meant separation from my family.

I was by then a Superintendent, having had some accelerated promotion, and I had been given a far-flung independent command. After a brief while, when my junior officer was removed, I was the only European policeman in the territory. I had a first-class African Inspector and an excellent team of NCOs.

I spent most of my time travelling around the stations, visiting the men of my police units, which were normally based on the administrative stations. This meant that I could get out and away into the 'real' Africa, while enjoying at the same time a fairly civilized base – blisteringly hot as it usually was – in Tamale.

Here was the usual Europeans-only Club, and here lived representatives of not only the Government departments, but also of the several trading firms that operated in the Gold Coast.

Tamale was the headquarters of the administration and I was there to greet one of the most remarkable figures of the African and, later, the Middle East colonial administrations, W.H. (Harold) Ingrams, our new Chief Commissioner.

He arrived in the unconventional manner that was a part of his stock in trade. He crossed the Sahara desert in a Ford van with his wife, children, nurse, secretary etc. When I knew him he was writing his book about this journey.

The Africans of this huge sun-blistered area, cut off from the south by the great rainforest belt that stretched right across central Africa, were of diverse tribal origins. They appeared in my time to be but little affected by politics and by a thirst for independence.

By now it was 1947 and India, that cornerstone of Empire, was suffering the divisions that resulted in the setting up of the separate independent republics of India and Pakistan.

That was, of course, meat and drink to the Nationalist elements in the Colonies. Down in the south of the Gold Coast, the population was becoming very clamant. Even so, the people of the Northern Territories seemed so far to be but little involved in such matters, and they pursued peacefully their normal agrarian life in the same manner that they had done for centuries.

One day in Tamale, B.B. Waddy's house was burgled and his sacred Harlequin cap, which was hanging on a wallstand peg, was stolen. B.B. was, of course, very upset.

In due course, one of our police patrols arrested a young African riding a bicycle through the streets of Tamale, with a Harlequin cap worn jauntily on his head. The burglar who had flogged the cap to the youth was soon traced. The latter had merely been the unknowing receiver of a very attractive piece of headwear.

I couldn't help regretting the disappearance from our Tamale streets of the impudent black youth with the colourful and prestigious headgear that he sported with such innocence.

'Dis man,' proclaimed the villager on my first arrival, indicating a worried-looking friend of his, 'he say some big big pussy cat go it him ship, and pliss you go kill-um.' I wasn't entirely sure of the lingo, but I was confident the man meant that a lion was eating goats (sheep) and would I please shoot it. We never caught up with the lion, which must have roamed away out of the area.

I was in Bawku, on the north-eastern tip of the territory. It was a place where things sometimes happened to gird the loins of a young man in search of adventure, even though fun and games had to be sandwiched between rather mundane official duties.

There was, for example, the occasion when a lion leapt

over me while I was lying on my camp bed on a flat Bawku rooftop. The lion had spotted a more attractive breakfast in the shape of a goat and I was in its path.

Then there was the business of the other lion that was feeding off the livestock of a village. Policemen being expected to deal with all breaches of the peace, I was petitioned to go after the beast and shoot it. Thus I set off across that blistering scrub and after a day-long trek I was forced to admit defeat. The lion was always one step ahead of me.

It was on the first of my lion-hunting expeditions that I became involved in the introduction of cricket to Bawku.

The District Commissioner had gone on leave and had written me a note because his replacement had been delayed and because, as an ardent evangelist of the game, he was anxious about the future of his trainees in Bawku. Knowing that I would shortly be up there on my police rounds, he asked if I would give his cricket fledglings the once over.

Having arrived in Bawku, and having calmed down the people who were so fussed about the 'Big Big Pussy Cat', I went through the usual parade formalities with the Inspector in charge of the unit. He had just been on a course in Britain, and had been taken to the Trooping of the Colour, which had impressed him enormously. However, his loyal enthusiasm had become overstrained, and instead of giving me a General Salute, which my status warranted, I got a Royal one.

Clearly I was in line for VIP treatment, because the 'cricket manager' sent to meet me called me 'Your Blessed Lordship'. He was an Afro/Asian, and I had heard that he enjoyed a drink or two.

I handed over to him a selection of cricket gear sent by the DC; this included the 'box', which hadn't so far reached that remote part of the world.

I turned to the Inspector, who wanted to talk about his London adventures. Suddenly there was a strangled noise behind me, and I found the 'manager' wearing the box over his face rather like a gas mask. His assistant had tied it on for him and had then gone off round the corner. The 'manager', gasping for air, was almost *in extremis* and urgently needed help. But the assistant had done a good job, and the knots were hard to untie.

At hand was my excellent senior sergeant, Salifu Dagarti (to die a good many years later whilst trying to defend Kwame Nkrumah during an attempted coup). He always kept his bayonet sharpened. It was the work of a moment, and the manager was free. I then tried to explain the mechanics of the box.

'Ah, I see,' said the manager, 'it will stop barl hitting barls.'

I had a large flask full of whisky and, because the manager was still spluttering, I rather rashly said, 'Help yourself,' and turned back to the Inspector.

The manager took me at my word. There was my flask lying on the ground, empty, and the manager - beaming toothily - was being helped away by the assistant.

On my way to my makeshift quarters I passed the manager sprawled in a deck chair outside a house. He was asleep and wearing the box upside down outside his trousers.

Next day, although the manager had a distinct hangover, we put the cricket recruits through their paces, and I was able in due course to report to the DC that he appeared to have some promising material. But there was no opportunity to put my recruits to the test. Before I could arrange a grand opening fixture, I was called back to Tamale.

I was, all this while, watching the weather somewhat anxiously. Bawku's only access - on British territory - was over a culvert which, during the rainy season, was often six feet under water, thus precluding all motorized transport, though if you were so disposed you could here and there wade in and out of the place.

The only alternative if you were caught by the rains was a very long, circuitous trek through French territory. We had an arrangement with the French for our police unit to be supplied by this route.

The rains were imminent as an order came for me to get back to Tamale and I made a quick getaway, passing en route the incoming relief DC and his caravan.

Back in Tamale I received a command. There was a shortage of legal officers, and I was to prosecute our Northern Territory commital cases in front of a judge, who happened to be an old friend of mine from Cape Coast days, when he had been a magistrate. There was much amusement at my daily arival at court mounted on my roan stallion, pulling up outside the building rather like a rodeo performer.

I mentioned earlier that at Mount Scopus in Palestine we had been put through some elementary training in self-defence and that one method had 'stuck' with me. It was at Zuarungu, outside the police station, that self-defence training I had gained in Palestine saved my life.

Suddenly a large African waving a *panga* (cutlass) came from nowhere, screaming abuse, and making straight for me. Somehow, automatically, I went for his cutlass arm, overturned him and jumped on him, just to make sure. It was the work of split seconds, and to this day I am surprised that the training of so many years before worked in an actual emergency. Anyway, he had a broken arm as a result of his attack on me. We got him fixed up, and I went to see him at the clinic.

His story was that some years earlier, down in the south, his wife had been violated by a white man. He had brooded, and suddenly everything had burst. I was the only white man in sight, and he had gone berserk.

My time in the Gold Coast was running out. In November 1947 the Commissioner, troubled by the political discord in the south, which was centred on Accra, transferred me from the NTs to take command of the Accra police.

Before leaving for Accra, I was joined by B.B. Waddy and Stuart Hordern, my police relief in Tamale. There was a 'rogue' elephant playing havoc among villagers and wrecking their crops. It had killed a woman. B.B. had been asked to go and shoot it, and wanted me to accompany him; Stuart said he'd come, too.

There had been a night's entertainment at the Tamale Club to send me on my way, which finished at about 3 a.m. and we had to be away after the elephant by 5 a.m. In the afternoon we had attended the annual Tamale 'Turf Meeting', where I rode in three races – one of them for a £5 wager. I had bet Charles Bowen, Colonel of the 2nd Battalion, that if he rode my roan horse 'Butler', I would ride the big black stallion that had just arrived from French country. I believed I would win. In the event I couldn't get my animal to make a proper start and, amid cheers from the Regiment, Charles and Butler came home in a canter about half a circuit ahead. I paid up.

It had all been a bit of an anticlimax. From 5 a.m. we walked and we walked, and so did the elephant; it was clear that it was ahead of us, going strongly and leading us into some fairly wild country. At around 12.30 p.m. we gave up the chase, much to the relief of Stuart, who wasn't used to this sort of thing (though as a Mosquito pilot over German-occupied France, he'd encountered infinitely worse things), and he'd been badly shaken when a hartebeest crashed out of the scrub almost on top of us. My memory throughout this episode is of B.B. Waddy, his heavy 450 express rifle over his shoulder, marching grimly ahead, clearly as dedicated to the job in hand as he always was on the cricket field, and impervious to the plaints of Stuart, who wanted to know, 'How much longer do we carry on this jamboree?'

It was a good question, and one that was very germane to my last few months in Accra. I was involved in an attempt to combat full-scale riots, which became an international *cause célèbre.* A number of people lost their lives, the world press had a field day, and I was sent on leave – though my actions were completely approved by a Commission of Enquiry – never to return to the colony. I was commended, given a decoration, and posted to Kenya.

It is a story that I have told at length elsewhere, and I won't weary my readers with the detail. At the time I was inclined to think it wasn't quite cricket, but then as someone said, 'What is life, if it isn't a game of cricket?'

12

Kenya Cameo

Who can accuse of covetousness the early travellers who first came to East Africa and saw - unbelievably - athwart the Equator the two monumental snow-capped peaks of Kenya and Kilimanjaro, framed by vast tracts of seemingly empty territory just waiting to be exploited? Naturally enough, they would settle and create a white-man's dominion.

My vision of that lush, inviting country was formed over the 10 years of my appointment as Assistant Commissioner of Police in the 1950s. Yet it is a vision of a country made up, like one of those exciting cakes in the 'Billy Bunter' school hamper, of numerous contrasting layers - some delectable, others less so, and some thoroughly indigestible. But I must avoid politics and imperial history, about which I have written extensively in other contexts.

It is the backdrop to my favourite game that concerns me here, the atmosphere, the climate, the life style.

Along the sea-girt littoral of Kenya there were the most wonderful sun-filled beaches. Some enterprising people had moved in and built places where one could laze, sunbathe and eat, astonishingly well, largely of freshly-caught fish. Here was a glorious holiday arena to which settlers and others flocked as and when they were able. There were indeed, up and down the coast between the Somalia border in the north and Tanganyika in the south, some hotels, particularly at Malindi, 100 miles north of

Mombasa, which – of their particular kind – would hold their own anywhere in the world.

The second, less inviting layer, going north, was a huge belt of very hot and arid thorn bush country, the abode of wild animals and mosquitoes. My wife Elaine, who was never well in the 'hot' tropics, called this 'The Hideousness'. In Mombasa, however, we were not very far removed from the foothills of Kilimanjaro, just over and across the Tanganyika border.

It was to a well-run German hotel at some 5,000 feet above sea level that Elaine and I sometimes repaired for a short 'break' from the humid coast.

There, too, well inland in the Teita region, was a range of hills where a few whites grew roses and other blooms that were good enough for any horticultural show. Near the top of the Teitas, one needed a fire to keep warm. The Africans of this area were markedly lighter in colour than elsewhere in Kenya. Presumably there must have been a European admixture somewhere back in the mists of time.

Next, still ascending steeply to the north, there was a thinning of the bush until it gave way, in the environs of Nairobi, to some lovely parklands reminiscent of shire Britain at its uncluttered best. I never knew, apart from brief visits, the essentially settler domains of the Rift Valley and Nyanza, which were scenically glorious.

Still ascending, there were the thick, dense, black rain forests of the Kenya and Aberdare ranges. These in turn gave way to the huge belt of bamboos, until finally one emerged onto the open plateau at about 12,500 feet, where the sun beat down in its full intensity, and where grew enormous lobelia, ferns and perennial flowers.

Finally, as one approached towards the final pyramid of Mount Kenya across this boggy moorland, there were the snows and glaciers and the biting cold of a climate that was far removed from the humidity of the coast, some 400 miles away. Up here, frozen into a glacier and clearly visible, is the body of a leopard that must have been trapped up there many years ago. Kenya is certainly a country of enormous contrasts.

It was a wonderful place to be, yet for reasons that I could never quite comprehend, my memories of it have never been entirely pleasurable. I was there during the Mau Mau 'troubles', but I was never seriously involved with them; and I became fascianted by the famous Errol murder, the 'Murder of the Century' as I have called it elsewhere*. And it all started off with a promising telephone call, within days of my arrival.

'Is that you, Skip?' came a voice that was vaguely familiar from the mists of the past.

It was 'Sailor' Oliver, with whom I had been a police 'rookie' at Mount Scopus in Palestine back in 1935. He was in Nairobi, and we arranged to meet.

There was 'Sailor' as large as life, still a very fine-looking man, and by all accounts still very well able to call his own tune with the ladies. Indeed, he was staying with one of his many conquests, but was on his way down to Australia, where he was hoping to catch up with another with whom he'd been in correspondence for years. We went to the Nairobi races, where we won some money. He didn't say much about his affairs since leaving the Palestine Police, but I feel sure they would have made a story worth hearing. He seemed prosperous enough. I believe that we exchanged a couple of letters after he departed, but then there was silence. I heard later that 'Sailor', still in Australia, had gone into seclusion. I found it difficult to believe it of so extrovert a character, but anything could happen to a man like 'Sailor'. However I have just learned of his death.

Of course, it wasn't long before I began to think of cricket.

Cricket, ah cricket. What a country in which to cultivate the greenest of velvet outfields and flat true wickets, and to play the game in conditions which only England in the benignest of summers could match.

But Kenya in colonial times was a place apart. There was plenty of cricket, but it was more or less confined to the

---

* See my *Policeman in Africa*.

privileged white communities that owned and occupied the fine clubs and country houses that abounded, and the Asian community that boasted some of the best cricketers and worst playing conditions. Seldom were non-Whites able to play on equal terms against the best of the white clubs. Thus the standard was seldom as high as it might have been, and it never vied with the lands of the Nawabs and Khans and emancipated slaves, where the chief legacy of colonial rule was invariably, almost mystically, an obsession with the masters' game.

The 'MCC' of the country were the Kenya Kongonis, and they organized and superintended the game, as well as running an annual tour of southern Britain, when – presumably – they had to co-opt players from members of the Club who were home on leave. I played twice in Sussex for the Kongonis.

There were some fine European cricketers in the country, But they were scattered around the territory and were rarely able to practice against comparable opposition. The grounds of both the Nairobi Club and the Sports Club in Mombasa were quite excellent in every way, and well worthy of cricket at its best. The settlers' club in Nairobi was called the Muthaiga, and this was lauded as being the only Kenya club to which a self-respecting European should belong. Twice I was invited as a 'guest' at the Muthaiga, but I found the Nairobi Club, which was open to anybody – including the 'also rans' – far more attractive. I have a feeling that the Muthaiga's reputation derived mainly from the wild orgies that, according to local legend, were the *raison d'être* of the club.

I played in Nyeri on a number of occasions, and it was there that I was once given out, caught at the wicket off my head from a short delivery that rose up like a ground-to-air missile. I was removed, stunned and cursing, to the sidelines. To this day I swear that bat never came within 12 inches of the ball. I had been going strongly for my 50, what's more.

I played most of my cricket in Mombasa, where there were

two European clubs – the Sports Club and the 'Stragglers'. I played at times for both, though at the Sports Club the cricket was by far the better of the two. It was run by one 'Taffy' Gallanders, once – though not in my time – of the Palestine Police Force XI at its splendid zenith. His enthusiasm and personal ability did much for the game in Mombasa.

I am convinced that a full Asian side would have beaten the Europeans, though so far as I am aware such a contest never took place.

Down in Mombasa, however, we were visited by a strong Asian touring side that included several Pakistan representative players. They were far too good for the local team, though I recall an excellent young cricketer, Peter Prodger, batting very well against some top-class spin bowling.

At the Club one evening, I got into conversation with a visitor who was passing through en route to South Africa. He was a little pink-faced pippin of a man, and he was no youngster. I gathered that he had something to do with the church, but no further information came my way and I didn't enquire. It was very evident that he had cricket in his blood, and we talked a lot about it. Finally I said that if he'd like a game, I could probably get him fixed up.

And so it came about.

He turned out in the colours of the Incogniti and said he once used to bowl. In due course our skipper invited him to bowl, having been assured by me that he had bowled in the past. Having placed an immaculate field, he pranced up to the wicket and – to the astonishment of batsmen and fielders alike – delivered the ball under-arm. His length was superb, and he could turn the ball both ways. I think his first victim gave himself up, standing with open mouth and immobile bat at the sound of falling timber. The incoming batsmen evidently thought the best way to deal with him was to put him off his delivery by thrashing him. But his field placing was much too cunning for that. Nobody could read him, there were several stumpings, and when bat was put to ball it almost invariably led to a dolly catch at some obvious place like short mid-off or mid-on, or cover point. Our side won easily.

It was the one and only time I encountered an under-arm bowler, though once at Malvern I saw the great Simpson-Hayward at work. He must by then have been getting on in years. He had played five times for England against South Africa in 1909.

Anyway, there I was saddled with my cricketing acquaintance who had had 'to do' with the church, and I handed him over to my ordained friend, John Cheese. When I later asked about him, all Cheese would say was, 'Alas, poor man.'

I never did discover whether my pick-up had been perhaps a recalcitrant verger, or even a defrocked priest. Never mind, he was an excellent cricketer, and one of the 'Old School'.

13

Postscript

Wandering from place to place in Asia and Africa, the world always seemed to me to resemble a village. You only had to get out and about, rather like walking up to the local pub, and lo and behold there popped up somebody you hadn't seen for ages.

Today as then, the chance meeting always seems to be the best. I never cease to be astonished at what unfolds.

It was in Mombasa that I was visited one morning by Harold Ingrams, my very senior officer when he was Chief Commissioner of the Northern Territories of the Gold Coast. He was now travelling in an official capacity on some special business that took him to a number of places in Africa and the Middle East.

I believe he had some private anxieties, and he seemed to be a somewhat unhappy man. He was in constant pain, having had a leg amputated in World War One. I later read several of his books, of which the best known and least esoteric was *Arabia and the Isles.*

His work was often of a nature that goes by the name of 'Special Duty' in both FO and military circles. He has been dead some 25 years as I write these words, and because I feel he never received the recognition that was his due in life, I would like to add a few words from the obituary written by Eric Macro, a friend of many who ventured into the Arab lands, and a kindly man I recall from my single meeting with him; Wing Commander Macro as he was in World War Two.

The Sudan was my first love . . . and it was in Khartoum that I first saw *Arabia and the Isles.* I asked Douglas Newbold, Civil Secretary of the time, if he knew 'this chap Ingrams.' 'That chap, as you call him,' said Newbold, 'will be a very big boy one day . . .' We had met first in that august Maida Vale drawing room where Dora Philby held court. Here, young and old alike, for Philby was remarkably tolerant of us striplings, would come to pay homage and be ushered into the presence . . . Harold had brought a token gift of real green Mocha coffee beans picked by his own hands in the hills near Mocha, the terraces behind Bait al-Faqih . . . We corresponded intermittently for thirty years or more, and occasionally would meet in Great Smith Street or the Athenaeum when we were both in England . . . In his quiet way he would rant on about what we were or weren't doing in Aden, but he really felt that the English had taken the wrong turning in South Arabia long before the war . . . Like Philby he was often a voice crying in the wilderness, and Whitehall paid scant heed to his warnings about our future in Aden and the protectorates . . . His work in the Hadhramaut gave birth to the catch-phrase 'Pax Ingrams', which has long since passed into our history books. I believe his talents were ill used, unrewarded and damned by faint praise by an ungrateful and ungracious Whitehall.*

To that, of course, many an unrecognized servant of the Raj will say *Amen.* When I met him in Africa his passion for Arabia had subsided somewhat. He remained for me a man of enormous ability and stature. Incidentally, for readers unfamiliar with the politics of Arabia, H. St John Philby (known in government circles as Hajji Philby) was the self-appointed advocate of the Saudi cause, a massively

* *Journal of Central Asian Society*, June 1974, p 236.

opinionated and prejudiced historian of the Middle East and, needless to say, father of Kim.

I was in London and it was 1945, and I was home on leave from the Gold Coast. We had passed on from VE Day, and VJ Day was approaching, but nobody then knew just how close it was. I was restless; it seemed to me that my own personal war, spent wholly in West Africa, had been far too easy and passive. I contrasted this with the experiences of my friends.

I went to some offices in Queen Anne's Gate, where I knew there was an organisation tee-ing up for re-entry into Malaya. Ushered into an office, I was confronted by a monocled, florid, grey-haired man in uniform, wearing the badges and red tabs of a full colonel. I recognized him at once: it was Aubrey Wallich, last seen at Kota Bahru in 1929.

I explained myself and then we talked about the Malaya we both had known and about its present plight under the Japanese. Aubrey had been away in India when the Japanese invasion occurred.

'Any news of A.K.?' I asked.

'Unhappily, no,' replied Aubrey. 'We fear he must be dead. There's been no news, so far as I'm aware, for several years. He was last heard of in central Asia, where he was doing a special job, but he vanished and there's been no news since.'

'And Sniffy Clark?' I asked.

'I just don't know,' said Aubrey, 'and I haven't been able to find out. I fear he must have been taken prisoner, and I doubt whether he would have survived a Jap prison camp.'

And then it came. I wanted an active job, Aubrey understood, and of course I knew Johore. Aubrey's team was looking for volunteers to drop into the jungle behind the Jap lines in order to liaise with the allied forces that were to invade Singapore. How did I feel about it? My martial ardour began to evaporate.

Even so, Aubrey and I had a very pleasant lunch, talking mainly about cricket. He'd been trying to start a club in his present office, 'But they're just an idle lot of bastards,' he said ruefully. 'They just don't seem to understand the importance of the game.'

It was the old Aubrey talking, just as when I last saw him at Kuala Krai. He had a Military Cross from World War One, and he received an OBE for his World War Two services. He never lost touch with Malaya. He died in 1960.

It would have been in the very late 1950s in a London bar. I hadn't noticed the barman until a voice said, 'It's a long way from bloody Kuala Lumpur.'

There was no mistake, it was 'Bloody' Matthews. I had last seen him in Jerusalem in 1935.

When he'd finished his shift we went for lunch and talked. He'd left the Palestine Police, and when war started he enlisted in the Tank Corps and found himself in North Africa.

'D'you know what they did to me?' he asked. 'Shot me in the bloody bottom, and I've never been the same since.' Anyway, he was still very much the same Matthews.

'Been bloody married twice,' he said, 'but I'm on my own now.' I think he was a lonely and somewhat unhappy man. He had never been 'one of us', as Sniffy or A.K. might have said. He had never to my knowledge held bat or ball in his hands, but now he had joined a club 'down Streatham way'. He wasn't very good, he said, but he got down there on Saturday afternoons and sometimes on a Sunday, and he enjoyed a few pints with the lads. 'You were always on about cricket,' he said, 'and now I've got the bloody bug.' It was the last I was to see of him.

I have already mentioned N.J.A. (Johnnie) Foster, the youngest of the seven Foster brothers, who in 1925 captained Malaya in an epic victory over the Australian touring side.

Now, soon after the end of the war, on the Sussex County ground at Hove, I was introduced to him and I was to get to know him a little over the next two or three years.

A large exuberant man, I think he was rather lonely. With an ever-present crony, he spent most of his time during the summer months watching any and every cricket match, from the top to the lowest class. Indeed, I recall an afternoon when the final ball of the season had been bowled. Johnnie rose from his seat and asked, as if it was the most obvious question in the world, 'What are we all going to do now?'

He was proud of being one of the cricketing Fosters. I remember an occasion when a strong Rhodesian touring team was playing against the Sussex Martlets. I happened to know the Rhodesian tour manager and introduced him to Johnnie. 'Not one of *the* Mr Fosters?' he asked.

Johnnie was delighted by the implied compliment and took him into the pavilion and gave him a guided tour of the photographs hanging on the walls of the pavilion lounge. 'My brother R.E. . . . My brother M.K. . . .' etc.

But Johnnie was restless and couldn't settle. I accompanied him one day to the Crystal Palace for the final of the Arthur Dunn football cup, which, that year, was between Malvern and Repton. I remember that Johnnie disapproved strongly of the very vocal supporters on both sides.

He often talked about his father, the Reverend Henry, and his mother Sophie. And he told me many a tale of the famous brothers; of the eldest H.K., who played for Worcester at 17 and made 179; of W.L., a regular officer who fought in the Boer War and the Somali campaign; of R.E., who was a golf and cricket Blue and who played amateur football for England; of the actor B.S. (Basil), who played 'rarely' for Worcester; of G.N., another golf and cricket Blue who became private secretary to Ranjitsinhji back in princely India; of M.K.and of himself, both of whom went to Malaya and became planters.

I, like all the cricket enthusiasts who ever met him, wanted Johnnie to talk about the three brothers who captained Worcester after it became a first-class county in 1899; about R.E.'s centuries in both innings for the Gentlemen against the Players in 1900, and his first test match, when he scored 287 against Australia. Johnnie always obliged. He was keen to assert whenever he had the opportunity that his sister Jessie was the best bowler in the family. She married a housemaster at Malvern, W. Greenstock, and it is not surprising perhaps that their son J.W. was an outstanding slow left-arm bowler and, in the tradition of the maternal side of the family, gained cricket and football Blues.

And naturally he talked of Malvern, where he and his brothers always covered themselves in glory. I remember, as a relatively new boy at Malvern, seeing three of the Fosters play against the school: H.K., resplendent in MCC colours, cover-driving with beautiful timing; G.N., an immaculate stylist in his Harlequins cap; M.K.,then the County captain, purposeful, seldom taking a chance even against schoolboy bowling.

At school reflected glory had come to me unexpectedly. I was 'up town' in Malvern when a car stopped alongside me. The driver handed me a note and said, 'I am Maurice Foster. When you go back to school, go to the pavilion and give this note to my brother Harry.' I did as I was bidden, but with some trepidation for I felt that I moved among the Lord's Elect and that fate had picked me out to be a heavenly messenger.

They were 'Mr Foster' to a man, and even to this day I find myself using their handle or their initials deferentially, as if they were as a family a cut above the rest of humanity, *sui generis.*

Eventually Johnnie went back to Malaya for a while, but that didn't work out, and finally he returned to Malvern, where he died in 1978, aged 88.

Considering that he had served in World War One (he had an MC and was twice mentioned in Dispatches), had lived for years in the enervating climate of Malaya, and had survived three years in a Japanese internment camp, he must have been a very tough 'cookie', but I remember him as a gentle soul.

For years during the 70s it had been my habit, and my great

pleasure, to walk the Sussex end of the South Downs. I would be out sometimes twice or thrice weekly, and I loved it. On this particular occasion I was coming down into the valley near Alfriston. I had strayed off the track and found myself in somebody's garden.

A voice said, 'Good morning, can I help you?' – and there was a tall craggy man with a shock of white hair. I explained myself, and he asked me into his house for a gin. He looked hard at me, and I at him.

'Haven't I seen you before?' he asked. 'Never forget a face.'

It was A.K., returned apparently from the dead. We talked and talked, during which time his very much younger wife came in.

I told of my meeting with Aubrey Wallich. 'Good fellow, A.W.'

I found myself back in the Singapore Cricket Club, where A.K. reigned supreme in the Synod.

'Yes, most people thought I was dead. Nearly was once or twice. Had to change my name. D'you remember Laverton? Good man that – right ideas; ran into him not so long ago in London. Found the fellow in one of those expensive restaurants; been the manager there for years and still had the run of the place. Fat as a pig . . .'

He seemed to reflect for a moment or two, then he said: 'Curious, this meeting of ours. I'd noticed through the window two squirrels fornicating at the end of the lawn, and I came out to have a closer look. It was then I saw you.'

It was the same old A.K., talkative, laconic, yet inscrutable. Later I introduced Elaine to him and his wife, and we met occasionally before he died in his eighties. Sadly, his wife was killed not long afterwards in a car accident.

A.K. never expanded upon the extraordinary life he'd obviously led in central Asia, and it wasn't for me to try and draw him.

Things for me had gone full circle. I was back on a visit to

Malvern, and was sitting in the pavilion watching a match between Malvern and Shrewsbury. Malvern were batting, and a shaggy-looking young man in somewhat soiled 'whites' and wearing a school football cap, went to the wicket laughing gaily and waving to his friends.

Shaggy or not, he knew how to play good aggressive cricket, and hit up a number of runs very quickly. Memories came flooding back of my own time at the school. I recalled the tall resplendent, perfectly accoutred figure of E.R.T. (Erroll) Holmes, later of Oxford, Surrey and England, in all his gallant splendour, striding down the bank on to the 'Senior' to make one of his dazzling centuries.

I recalled, too, the very immaculate Charles Fiddian Green, the cricket master of my time, who always insisted on proper 'turn-out' by all boys who aspired to play cricket. He had played against Oxford at Lords in the very powerful Cambridge XI of 1921, under the captaincy of Gilbert Ashton, whose two brothers, Hubert and Claude, were also in the side. I believe that Charles had also turned out on occasion for both Warwickshire and Worcestershire.

As I have already recorded, I played club cricket at Seaford under H.L. Wilson, sometime captain of Sussex, and at Hendon, under C.J.T. Poole, who had captained Northants. Both were sticklers for clean and orthodox turn-out. The latter indeed had once taken me to task – and very rightly – for dirty boots and a muddy bat.

I glanced at an elderly companion in the pavilion, who had been sitting impassively, but who was now making a wry face.

'Things have changed too much for me,' he said. 'I've lived mostly at Malvern for over 70 years, and I'm now moving elsewhere.' That was Cyril Lace. I hadn't known him very well, but at nearly 90 he had become Malvern's 'Grand Old Man'. He died shortly afterwards.

I see him and all the others as clearly now as I saw them in the steamy heat of Malaya, or the 'cool' seasons of Palestine, or the jungle clearings of Africa, or the green pastures of an English summer; lined up in my private pantheon like

Greek gods. For those who knew them, or who are familiar with the conventions of the scorecard, initials are usually enough: W.G., A.K., A.W., R.G.B., M.K., H.K., etc. Sometimes it's an affectionate nickname that has pursued its owner from school to posterity, that persists in the memory, like 'Sniffy' Clark; or a sobriquet like 'The Don' or 'The Master', which we recognize more instinctively than Sir Donald or Sir Jack.

I hope that I have not overplayed the 'mystical' element of cricket, because after all, the game itself can be such fun. Accordingly I would like to finish on a light note with three small anecdotes.

THE CRITICS

For a number of years I was a member of the MCC, that august body, and was thus well acquainted with the rites - mystical or otherwise - that went on in the pavilion at Lords. Of course, all county memberships have their critics, but the tradition is that the Lords critics are the ancestors of them all. Certainly, they used to rule the roost at Lords, and probably still do. Critics are usually - though not always - old gentlemen who may well have been prominent in cricket circles for many years. They air their views vehemently to each other, and sometimes to others who may not be within their own charmed circle. They discuss in considerable detail the merits and demerits of current playing cricketers, comparing them - usually to their disadvantage - with the giants of the past. Then, as likely as not, they fall asleep with panama hat over nose; the sheer effort of it all had been just too much.

I always wished that the critics could be labelled, so that one would know just who they were. Most of them, with a look of stern disapproval on their faces about anything and everything, are to be seen wearing a faded 'old' pattern MCC tie, the colours of which are startling. I have had one or two of these critics pointed out to me, and once gazed with awe and reverence at an imposing, craggy-looking figure who had in his day borne a cricket name that was household. Most playing cricketers come under close scrutiny: 'Old so-and-so would have made mincemeat of him,' they aver, nodding their hoary heads in agreement.

But one day we had a diversion. I was sitting just below the Long Room between two critics who talked across me. Suddenly there was a loud crash from behind us. Somebody went up to see what it was all about, and he came back looking grim. 'It's poor old Horsey Simpson – used to know him in India. Afraid he's had it – fallen off one of those tall stools he always sits on. Will lean forward – bound to collapse sooner or later, but maybe this is the way he'd want to go.' And with that, he went back for another look. Returning 10 minutes later with a broad grin, he said, 'It's all right, Horsey is sitting up, asked for the score.'

A CRICKET CURIOSITY

It was after World War Two and I was on leave. General Sir Miles Dempsey, who had commanded the British Army during the Allied re-entry into Europe in 1944, used to run a cricket side that toured parts of Mid-Sussex, playing against villages and clubs. I played in several of those games, and it was 'small' cricket at its best. We had heard about the fame of a certain bowler, known to all as 'The Little Sod'. In this particular match, I was one of the openers and took first ball. With black hair flying, in came the Little Sod off a run of about 14 paces. He was fast-medium, and for four balls I played him without much difficulty. Then came the fifth ball of the over. I was quietly fidgeting at the crease, as batsmen do, waiting as he went back for his run-up. Suddenly, however, he turned, after only a couple of steps, and delivered the ball fast and straight. I hadn't time to stand aside or to offer a stroke, and my stumps were in disarray. I was so surprised that I didn't even appeal – I just 'walked'. As I passed deep mid-off, he said, ''E does that quite often, does The Little Sod. No 'ard feelings.' The

General said, 'What was that all about?' Bemusedly I said that I really didn't know. Anyway we were forewarned. We had an Oxford Blue playing for us, and in making his century he simply took The Little Sod apart, and wrecked his season's average.

A MEMORY OF F.R. (FREDDIE) BROWN

At Horsham on an intermittently rainy day. I was in attendance at a boys' match in which my son was playing. Between showers I conversed with a large cheerful man, whose boy was also playing. I remember giving him a long and highly instructive lecture on the subject of cricket, at which he was thoughtfully silent. The cricket was at last abandoned and my acquaintance departed, saying he was off to Worplesdon to play some golf. I learnt just afterwards that I had been talking with F.R. (Freddie) Brown (1910-1991) a cricket captain of England, who had played cricket for Surrey and Northants and become President of MCC 1971-72.

I count my blessings, for to have seen the greatest of them, to have played alongside some, and to have conversed with many, is a rich enough picking for any man in the brief moment of our life on earth.